How to Live—and Die—With

Colorado
Probate

Gulf Publishing Company
Book Division
Houston, London, Paris, Tokyo

How to Live—and Die—With

Colorado Probate

Wills, Trusts, and Estate Planning in Layman's Language

L. William Schmidt, Jr.

How to Live—and Die—With
Colorado Probate

ISBN 0-87201-118-6

Library of Congress Cataloging-in-Publication Data

Schmidt, L. William.
  How to live—and die—with Colorado probate.

  Includes index.
  1. Probate law and practice—Colorado—Popular works.
I. Title. II. Title: Colorado probate.

KFC1944.Z9S   1985   346.78805'2   85–21923

ISBN 0-87201-118-6   347.880652

**This book is published with a grant from the Trust
Group of Central Bank of Denver.**

Contents

Dedication

This book is dedicated to my mother, Violet K. Schmidt, and in loving memory of my father, Lail W. Schmidt, without whose sacrifice and example there would be no book.

Preface

The law of estate planning and probate—the law dealing with transmission of property from a decedent to his beneficiaries—is centuries old, yet little understood. Every adult citizen should understand the purpose of probate and the people it protects, and with this understanding be motivated to plan his or her estate.

Every effort has been made to interpret in this book, fully and fairly, major facets of estate planning and probate—to present the subject in a well-balanced and readable form. This book is not intended to be a "do-it-yourself" substitute for carefully made estate plans. On the contrary, it is intended to point up the folly of homemade wills and amateur decisions about probate. General principles have been stated to provide an overall view of the subject. The reader with expertise will notice that certain exceptions to general rules have been omitted. The author felt that the reader should have an understanding of general principles, unencumbered by exceptions. Thus, the importance of personal consultation with legal counsel proficient in the fields of estate planning and probate cannot be overemphasized.

The author wishes to acknowledge the assistance of Denver attorneys Barbara J. Parker, Kenneth T. Eichel, Peter R. Moisen, and Harley K. Look for their assistance in the preparation of certain portions of this book.

The author also wishes to acknowledge with gratitude a grant from the Trust Group of Central Bank of Denver which provided all of the costs in connection with the publication of this book.

A special thanks to the State Bar of Texas, whose book on Texas probate was the inspiration and model for this book, and to Charles A. Saunders, a partner in the Houston law firm of Fulbright & Jaworski, who was the editor of the Texas book and who encouraged me to prepare this material for the education of the people of Colorado in the vital matters of estate planning and probate.

1

What Is Probate?

The Word "Probate"

The word "probate" originally meant "to test and to prove." It came to mean the procedure of establishing before a court of proper jurisdiction that an instrument is the last will and testament of a deceased person.

In Colorado, probate has come to include not only the determination by the probate court that an instrument is the last will and testament of the decedent, but the doing of all those things which the probate court has jurisdiction to do in settling estates.

Probate proceedings involve determining whether the deceased left a valid will; appointing and qualifying a personal representative for the estate; collecting the assets of the estate; preparing an inventory of the estate; preparing estate, inheritance, and income tax returns; establishing and paying claims and taxes; selling property to pay debts or to effect distribution of the estate; determining those who are entitled to receive the property of the estate and distributing their property to them; settling the accounts of the personal representative; discharging the personal representative and releasing the sureties on his bond; and closing the estate.

Under the Colorado Probate Code, the probate court is the district court established for each county. The only exception is in the City and County of Denver where there is a court assigned to handle only probate matters called the Denver Probate Court. In some larger counties, a separate division of the district court handles only probate matters.

What Is a "Personal Representative"?

The personal representative of the estate of a deceased is the person authorized by the court to act for the estate. In some states, the personal representative is called an "executor" or an "administrator." He is appointed by the court and qualifies by signing an oath and giving bond, if a bond is required. Banks and corporations with trust powers, as well as individuals, may act in this capacity. The court will appoint as personal representative the person named in the will, unless some unusual reason compels a different appointment. The personal representative must make bond, unless the deceased has directed otherwise in his will or unless the personal representative is a bank with trust powers. The court may waive bond in certain cases.

The clerk of the court issues "letters" to a personal representative after he has been appointed by the court, has filed his oath of office, and has made any bond that may be required and approved by the court. "Letters" are a printed form certified by the court clerk that the holder is in charge of the estate and entitled to possession of the assets. Letters are evidence of authority to take charge of an estate and to act for it.

What Is the "Estate"?

The estate of a person includes everything he owns. In this sense a person's estate is the aggregate of all his assets, riches, and fortune, and includes rights to receive income from property owned by another. One of the common uses of the word is to denote and describe, in a most general manner, the property and assets of a deceased person.

The "probate estate" of a deceased person is that part of his property and assets which the personal representative of his estate administers and which is subject to the applicable laws and terms of the will and control of the court. It does not include any property or assets of the deceased which do not pass into the hands of the personal representative. The probate estate of a deceased person exists from his death until all debts have been paid, the property has been distributed, and the personal representative has been discharged.

The probate estate is not to be confused with the "gross estate," as gross estate is defined for purposes of assessing the federal estate tax. A deceased person may have owned or controlled property, or enjoyed income from property during his lifetime that is a part of his gross estate for tax purposes but is not a part of his probate estate. For example, the deceased during his lifetime may have disposed of certain assets which remain a part of his gross estate for tax purposes but not part of his probate estate. Common examples are:

1. Gifts made before the death of the donor. (However, most outright gifts to any one person in any one year of a total value of $10,000 or less will not be a part of the taxable estate.)
2. Conveyances of property in which the grantor reserved income or control for his lifetime.
3. Trusts created by a person who reserved the right to revoke, alter, or amend the trust or to control the beneficial enjoyment of the property or to receive income during his lifetime.

What Is Not Included in the Probate Estate?

The "probate estate" does not include all of the property and assets owned by a deceased person during his lifetime. Even a person of modest means usually owns property said to be a part of his estate but which does not pass under his will and never becomes a part of his probate estate. Such property may include insurance, employee benefits, social security, property in joint tenancy, and trust property.

Life Insurance

Life insurance is payable on a person's death in the manner provided by the policy. It is usually made payable to a named beneficiary, and in the case of the prior or simultaneous death of the beneficiary, it is made payable to a contingent beneficiary. The insured is usually the owner of the policy. The proceeds of such a policy are not payable to the personal representative of the estate of the insured and do not become a part of his probate estate. However, the proceeds will be a part of the probate estate of the insured if they are made payable to his estate by the terms of the policy or if all named beneficiaries die before the proceeds become payable. The proceeds are taxable if the decedent had an "incident of ownership" in the policy, or if it was payable to his personal representative.

Annuities and Retirement Benefits

An annuity may be payable under what is known as an "annuity contract" or under an insurance policy with provisions for payment of benefits during the lifetime of the insured and, perhaps, thereafter. An individual may be the beneficiary of an annuity created by a contract purchased by him or purchased by another for him. He may be an employee of a corporation which had a pension plan or profit-sharing plan under which he and his spouse or dependents are entitled to payments. He or his employer may have created an Individual Retirement Account (IRA), a Keogh Plan, or other "simplified" pension plan. Any amounts payable after the death of the beneficiary will be payable according to the terms of the annuity contract, insurance policy, or pension plan. In most cases the amounts payable after the death of the beneficiary will not become a part of his probate estate.

Social Security and Government Pensions

Social Security benefits and pensions payable under federal of state law do not become a part of the probate estate. These amounts may or may not be taxable. However, any amounts payable but not actually paid prior to the death of a beneficiary become payable to the personal representative of his estate as part of the probate estate.

Bonds

United States Savings Bonds may be made payable to the deceased as owner or co-owner, or to a beneficiary named by the decedent. If the co-owner or named beneficiary survives the deceased, the survivor is the absolute owner of the bonds. They do not become a part of the decedent's probate estate, although they may be included, in whole or in part, in his gross estate for tax purposes. Of course, these bonds will be a part of the probate estate of the surviving co-owner or named beneficiary if he still owns them at the time of his death and has not caused them to be reissued to himself and another person as a co-owner or to a named beneficiary.

Property in Joint Tenancy

Property owned by the deceased and another in joint tenancy with right of survivorship is not a part of the probate estate of the deceased. This property is often referred to as *jointly owned property*. It passes to the surviving joint tenant upon the death of the deceased joint owner by operation of law and the contract entered into when the joint tenancy was established. Many stocks, bonds, bank accounts, savings and loan accounts, and certain other properties are jointly owned. This assumes that the joint tenancy with right of survivorship was created in a valid manner.

Trust Property

Property conveyed by an individual to a trustee to be administered in trust and distributed after the individual's death usually is not a part of the probate estate. A person has a right to convey his property to a trustee to be held and administered in trust, with the income and property of the trust estate to be used and distributed as provided in the instrument. The grantor may make himself the trustee; he may reserve the right to alter, and amend, or revoke the trust during lifetime; he may make himself the beneficiary of the trust. The property of a trust of this kind generally would not be subject to administration by the personal representative and would not be a part of his probate estate, unless the trust terminated or was revoked by the grantor prior to death.

If the deceased was the trustee or beneficiary of a trust created by some other person, or if he was entitled to receive income from or use of property, these rights terminate upon death. The property in which he has these rights will not be part of the probate estate, except income payable to him or possibly other vested rights he had in the property at the time of his death.

Small Estate Transfers

Since probate administration under court supervision is only necessary to transfer title to property held in the sole name of a decedent, it is possible through the various forms of property ownership already discussed to eliminate the need for probate. However, even though the majority of the estate may have been held in a form to avoid probate, there may always be some property still titled in the name of the deceased owner. Colorado law provides for the transfer of a certain amount of property titled in the name of a decedent without the necessity of court procedures. Where the total value of all property, less liens and encumbrances, does not exceed $20,000, such property may be transferred to the person entitled to it simply by executing a written affidavit in the form prescribed by statute. This procedure may not be used to transfer title to real estate. This technique can be extremely useful, but it is not a substitute for careful planning where the total elimination of probate is a major consideration.

The Probate Process

The probate process has traditionally been a very complicated, time-consuming, and costly process that has been neither understood nor appreciated by the general public. It has been a breeding ground of much mischief. In 1974 Colorado adopted the Uniform Probate Code, which was a new system of probate designed to introduce choices in the probate process so that it could be greatly simplified in the majority of cases.

The first choice regards the manner in which the decedent's last will and testament is probated. If there is no contest regarding the validity of the will or any of its provisions, it is possible to have the will informally probated without the need for testimony by the witnesses to the will, and without the need for an official court determination of the validity of the will.

If for some reason any person interested in the estate of the decedent requests a formal determination regarding the validity of the will, notices are sent to all interested parties and a court hearing is held to examine the will and obtain an official judicial determination of its validity.

Obviously, the formal method is more costly and time-consuming, and it would presumably be used only in cases where there was an issue of validity. Issues of validity include questions as to the authenticity of the signature of the person making the will, questions regarding the mental capacity of the testator to make a valid will, and issues relating to possible physical or mental duress.

After the will has been admitted to probate, the individual or institution named in the will as the personal representative is appointed by the court to administer the estate. A formal notification of the court appointment called "letters" is issued as evidence of the authority of the personal representative. If there is no living and qualified personal representative named in the will, or if the decedent died intestate (without a will), the court will appoint a personal representative determined by a set priority based upon relationship to the decedent. The personal representative by exhibiting a certified copy of his letters can protect purchasers and others with whom he deals. Thus, as soon as letters are issued, the assets of the estate are completely marketable.

There are also choices with regard to the degree of formality with which the estate is administered by the personal representative. A formal administration, if requested by the beneficiaries or ordered by the court for the protection of the estate, involves most of the complexity and delay which existed under the law before the enactment of the Colorado Probate Code. All important actions on the part of the personal representative must be approved in advance by the court. Periodic accountings will ordinarily be required to be filed with the court. Formal probate would ordinarily not be desirable except in cases where there is a great deal of distrust or hostility among beneficiaries or between the beneficiaries and the personal representative.

Most probate proceedings in Colorado are under the informal administration alternative. Under this method of operation, the personal representative is enabled to possess and deal with the assets of a decedent or to distribute them to the persons who are entitled to them. Notice to creditors is published in a local newspaper, giving an opportunity for all persons to whom the decedent was indebted to file claims in the estate for payment of such debts. The personal representative reviews the claims and pays those which he feels are legitimate. Claims which are disallowed may be submitted to the court for determination. The personal representative is entitled to continue the business of the decedent and to act in a prudent manner to manage and deal with the assets of the estate.

After all claims, including taxes that may be due as a result of the death of the decedent, have been paid or provided for, the personal representative has the responsibility of distributing the remaining assets to the beneficiaries named in the decedent's will, and if there was no will, then to the statutory heirs of the decedent.

Although the administrative process may have initially been commenced informally, any person interested in the state may at any time petition the court to force a formal administration with all of the notice and hearings which result.

There are even options with regard to the eventual closing of the estate. This may be done informally by the personal representative filing with the court a sworn statement indicating that he has published the required notice to creditors, that all expenses of administration and claims have been paid, that the estate has been distributed to the persons entitled to the assets, and that a copy of the sworn statement has been sent to persons having an interest in the estate as a creditor or beneficiary. One of the disadvantages to this informal method of closing the estate is that the personal representative continues to be liable for his actions for one year after the filing of the closing statement.

On the other hand, the personal representative may decide to have a formal proceeding to terminate the administration of the estate by asking the court to approve a final accounting and to approve the final distribution of the estate to the beneficiaries. This requires notice be given to all interested parties and a hearing before the court. If the court is satisfied that everything has been properly administered, the request of the personal representative is approved and his liability terminates at that time.

The combination of choices for opening, administering, and eventually closing an estate are numerous. In a particular situation, it might be determined to have a formal probate of the will with an unsupervised or informal administration of the estate, followed by a formal closing. In most cases, however, especially where there is no conflict or disagreement among the beneficiaries of the estate, it is most expeditious and inexpensive to have an informal probate of the will, an unsupervised administration of the estate, and an informal closing based upon the sworn statement of the personal representative. Since the choices are so numerous, and since the consequences may be very important, it is essential to have the advice and assistance of qualified legal counsel.

Summary

Not everything a person owns or considers his property will become a part of his probate estate. Large parts of the estate often go to beneficiaries outside the will. Care, then, should be taken to make certain that a sufficient amount of property (probate estate) will pass under the will to pay estate debts, take care of legacies, and accomplish the purposes intended by the will. Moreover, property may be a part of the gross estate of a decedent for federal tax purposes regardless of whether it is a part of his probate estate.

2

What Will Probate Cost?

Of universal interest is the question, "What will probate cost my estate?" The answer involves careful consideration of the size, type, and location of the present and future assets comprising the estate income, any tax complications present, the simplicity or complexity of the disposition of the estate, the extent and type of the debts, and various other factors.

This chapter will deal with costs and expenses in relatively routine administrations. It will not cover probate intricacies in unusual situations or complicated probate litigation.

Court Cost and Bond Premiums

Court costs are set out in the state law and in schedules of charges published by the clerks reponsible for handling the court papers. Such costs include an initial docket fee of $75 to cover a wide variety of court services for administration of an estate. In addition, there will be other costs for certified copies of documents and other routine court expenses. The lawyer can make an accurate estimate of court costs once he knows whether there is provision for an independent executor, whether bond has been waived, the nature and extent of the decedent's assets, whether there is a probability of litigation, and similar facts.

No bond is required of a personal representative appointed in an informal probate proceeding unless the last will and testament requires the posting of a bond or unless a beneficiary or creditor makes a demand that bond be posted. Bond may be required by court order in a formal probate proceeding unless the last will and testament specifically relieves the personal representative of the bonding requirement. However, any person interested in the estate may still request that a bond be posted, and the court will then determine whether it feels that protection of the estate would require the posting of a bond.

If bond is required for any reason, the amount of the bond and its cost will depend upon a number of factors. The purpose of the bond, of course, is to protect the estate against negligent or improper actions on the part of the personal representative resulting in damage to or loss of estate assets. The Colorado Probate Code contains a number of provisions which permit the court to determine the amount of the bond and to determine whether or not security or surety should be provided in addition to the personal guarantee of the individual serving as personal representative.

Appraisal Fees

The personal representative may employ qualified appraisers to assist in determining the fair market value of any asset at the time of the decedent's death which may be subject to reasonable doubt. Different persons may be employed to appraise different kinds of assets included in the estate. The need for appraisals is especially important where there is real estate or an interest in a business. Depending upon the complexity of the property being appraised, the cost could range from a few hundred dollars to many thousands of dollars.

Personal Representative's Fees

Under the Colorado Probate Code, the personal representative is entitled to a reasonable fee. The statute does not set the fee.

This is contrary to the law as it existed before the enactment of the Code when there was a statutory fee schedule based upon a percentage of the value of the estate. If the will provides for the compensation of the personal representative, but there was no lifetime contract with the decedent by the personal representative regarding compensation, the personal representative may renounce the provision in the will and then be entitled to reasonable compensation. The personal representative may renounce his right to all or any part of the compensation by a written renunciation filed with the court. For the personal representative to avoid possible income and gift tax liability in connection with the waiver of compensation, he must make a clear and irrevocable renunciation of his right to receive the compensation.

Attorney Fees

The personal representative is entitled to employ attorneys, accountants, and any other agents that may be necessary to assist in the administration of the estate. These individuals are entitled to be paid a reasonable fee for their services. Although attorney fees in Colorado were once determined by applying a percentage figure to the total value of the property subject to probate, those fee schedules are no longer in effect. The attorney's fee is now regarded as a private matter to be agreed upon between the lawyer and client in accordance with proper standards of reasonableness. If a bank or trust company is acting as the personal representative, the services performed by the attorney for the estate will be fewer than if an individual family member is serving as personal representative. This is due to the fact that the bank or trust company will have the background and experience to perform many tasks which the attorney will need to perform if an inexperienced family member is handling the estate. Any beneficiary of the estate can request the court to review the reasonableness of attorney fees, or the court can review such fees on its own initiative.

What Is a Reasonable Fee?

The Colorado Probate Code sets forth certain factors to be considered as guides in determining the reasonableness of a fee. These factors would apply in determining the fee of the personal representative, the attorney for the estate, or any other agent of the estate. These factors closely follow the Canons of Ethics of the American Bar Association in describing the points to be considered in determining the amount of legal fees. The following factors are to be considered:

- The time and labor required, the novelty and difficulty of the questions involved, and the skill requisite to perform the service properly.
- The likelihood, if apparent to the personal representative, that the acceptance of the particular employment will preclude the person employed from other employment.
- The fee customarily charged in the locality for similar services.
- The amount involved and the results obtained.
- The time limitations imposed by the personal representative or by the circumstances.
- The experience, reputation, and ability of the person performing the services.

No one of these considerations in itself is controlling. They are merely guides in ascertaining the real value of services performed on behalf of the estate.

Summary

Colorado has led the way among American jurisdictions in streamlining its probate procedures to minimize probate costs and simplify the administration of decedents' estates by dispensing with formal court administration. With a proper will probate court costs are minimal, and there is no bonding expense. The fees of executors and administrators can be estimated once the gross value and nature of the estate and probable income and disbursements are known.

In Colorado, attorney fees for services to the executor or administrator are not set by law but are the subject of private agreement. If an attorney is required to set or estimate a fee in advance, he may suggest a small percentage figure based upon the estate's gross value. If an attorney is employed on a reasonable fee basis to be determined upon completion of his services, he may make a charge to an executor or administrator that will be less than an arbitrary percentage figure. Such a fee must be reasonable in light of all the considerations set out in the Canons of Ethics of the State Bar of Colorado. The fees of attorneys serving administrators under court control are subject to the approval of the probate court, and the court requires the attorney to prove the reasonableness of his charge. When a testator does not make a proper will, the cost of administering his estate will be higher than if a properly prepared will has been made by an attorney who was naturally familiar with expense-cutting provisions, meaning of legal terms, consequences of legal principles, requirements for executing wills, and the necessity for definiteness.

A person needing the services of an attorney should not hesitate to discuss his fee or any other cost of probate with him. Substantial savings of probate costs can be effected by proper planning.

3

When Is My Estate Valued and Why?

An estate is valued on several occasions and may be valued for several reasons. An initial reason is to obtain facts upon which to plan the most efficient and economical transfer of the estate to the persons who are to receive it after the death of the owner. The planning should be done during the lifetime of the owner of the estate. Taxes and expenses may be minimized to the extent permitted by law. The transfer may then be carried out according to the owner's wishes.

Therefore, the most important valuations of an estate are made during the owner's lifetime, when the owner can determine the disposition of the estate and can revise the plan as values or circumstances change. This is true whether the estate is large or small. The estates of both spouses should be valued in this planning stage. The owners can, by making these valuations, determine whether the estates consist of the desired kinds of properties and how far these properties will go in carrying out the desired intentions, whether the intentions are to protect a spouse, furnish an education for children, or for other purposes. These valuations afford opportunities for tax planning, as well as helping to determine the desirability of property exchange between spouses, equalizing their respective estates, or making lifetime gifts.

The owner, while living, has a free choice to decide how the transfer of the estate will be made. The owner may choose whether the order of descent and distribution of the estate will be determined by law, by the owner through transfer before death, in a will, or by other procedures that are available but can be used only if the owner elects to use them. Only by knowing values and purposes can the most efficient and economical transfer of properties be planned and achieved. These elections are made by every person, knowingly or unknowingly, when the individual makes a will, delays making a will, or simply decides not to make a will.

Valuations of an estate after the death of the owner are important under state and federal laws. The first valuation after death should include the probate and nonprobate estate subject to federal estate tax. Determination then can be made whether the federal estate tax laws apply. If they do, occasions for use of alternate valuations of an estate are provided by the tax laws.

Valuation for Tax Purposes

Regardless of any appraisal made during the course of proceedings under the Colorado Probate Code, there must be a valuation made of estates, whether large or small, for tax purposes. There is a practical as well as a legal necessity to demonstrate either that no taxes are due or that taxes due have been paid. This valuation is made to enable timely payment of any taxes due and the distribution of the estate to the beneficiaries free of any tax lien.

A return must be made to the Internal Revenue Service for federal estate tax purposes within nine months after the death of the decedent, depending on the value of the estate. If death occurred in 1985, a return is required if the gross estate (before any allowances for debts, expenses, or other permitted deductions) is in excess of $400,000; if during 1986, in excess of $500,000; and if during 1987 or thereafter, in excess of $600,000.

Values Six Months After Death

Using values as of six months after death is commonly referred to as using the "alternate valuation date." Under federal tax laws, the alternate valuation date can be elected by a personal representative. The purpose of this provision, born of the depression days of the 1930s, is to provide tax relief where there has been a decline in the values of an estate within six months after the decedent's death.

Properties acquired from a decedent generally take as a new basis for income tax purposes the value at the date of the decedent's death, or, if elected, the alternate valuation date, unless a permitted special-use valuation method has been elected. Electing the higher tax valuation of date of death or alternate valuation date may be advantageous for federal income tax purposes upon later sale or disposition of property received by the surviving spouse or other beneficiaries from the decedent's estate, as well as upon the later sale or disposition by the surviving spouse of his or her interest in community property.

One important exception to the stepped-up basis rule, among others, applies to property received by the decedent by gift within the one-year period before the decedent's death. If the person who gave the property to the decedent (the donor) reacquires the property from the decedent's estate, the basis of the property in the hands of the donor or donor's spouse will be the same basis which the decedent had before his death, although the property had a higher value at the decedent's death (or on alternate valuation date) and was subject to estate tax at the higher valuation. This exception prevents a donor from obtaining a stepped-up basis in property given to a decedent within the short period prior to the decedent's death to minimize the donor's income taxes on a subsequent sale by the donor (or his spouse) after reacquiring the property from the decedent's estate. The exception also applies when the donor (or donor's spouse) acquires the proceeds of a sale of such property made by the estate of the decedent.

The proper use of the alternate valuation date might likewise determine whether any federal estate taxes are due on the estate. Although filing of a federal estate tax return may be required based on date-of-death values, determination of tax to be paid is made on alternate valuation-date valuations if the election is made properly.

The alternate valuation date may be used only if there is a timely filing of the federal estate tax return and the election is made to use the alternate valuation date. Then all of the property in the estate must be valued as of the alternate date rather than the date of death (subject to a few special rules). However, if the alternate valuation date is used, then any property distributed, sold, exchanged, or otherwise disposed of within six months after decedent's death is valued at the value on the date of distribution or disposition. The value of any interest which is affected by a mere lapse of time, such as the paying out of an annuity or the expiration of a patent, is not entitled to be revalued where the revaluation reflects only the effect of the passage of time.

Special Use Valuations

The Tax Reform Act of 1976 introduced concepts of special-use valuations for relief to farmers and owners of closely held businesses. While these provisions are still in effect, the Economic Recovery Tax Act of 1981 (ERTA) made important changes applying to estates of persons dying after 1981.

If properly elected by the personal representative of the estate, qualified real estate (which is included in decedent's gross estate and used for farming purposes or in a closely held trade or business) may be valued for estate tax purposes on the basis of its value for its actual use instead of the fair market value for its highest or best use. For example, although a farm approached by urban expansion might have a higher market value for commercial development than for continued farming, it can be valued for estate purposes at its value as a farm rather than as urban development property. The reduction in gross estate values by such election, however, cannot exceed in the aggregate $750,000 where the decedent's death occurred in 1983 or thereafter.

For the election to apply after 1981, in addition to other requirements, the qualifying real property must have been used by the decedent or his family as a farm or in a trade or business; have been so used for at least five out of eight years prior to the decedent's death, disability, or retirement with material participation by the decedent or his family during such years; pass from the decedent to defined members of the family; have a value at least equal to 25% of the adjusted gross estate; and the value of the entire farm or business, including both real property and personal property used in farming or in the trade or business, must have a value equal to at least 50% of the decedent's adjusted gross estate. The valuations used for the 25% and 50% tests are values of the highest and best use, rather than the actual use. Computations of the value of the gross estate for these tests include gifts made by the decedent within three years prior to decedent's death. The inclusion of these gifts in the gross estate prevents death-bed gifts by the decedent of other property to qualify the farm or trade or business real property for the special use valuations. A farm for this purpose includes, among other things, ranches, nurseries, orchards, and, subject to other special rules, woodlands. The tax law provides a formula for determining the actual value of farms using the cash rental basis of comparable land, or if none, net share rental of comparable land, and other factors. Other methods may, however, be used for determining the actual value of the real estate used in farming or in the trade or business.

The estate tax benefits realized by these special use valuations may be recaptured by a tax imposed upon the recipients of the property from the decedent if within 10 years after the decedent's death the qualified property is transferred out of the defined family, or the property ceases to be used (with some exceptions) for the purpose for which the special use valuation was intended.

Disclaimer Valuations

Federal tax laws, as well as property laws of most states, including Colorado, permit a beneficiary of an estate to refuse to accept all or any part of a bequest or inheritance from a decedent by properly executing and filing a written disclaimer within nine months after the death of the decedent. The effect is to transfer the bequest or inheritance which is disclaimed to other persons who would have been the beneficiaries of such bequest or inheritance had the person disclaiming been deceased on the death of the decedent. This procedure, in effect, permits a tax-free transfer by the disclaiming beneficiary to another, for example, from a surviving spouse to children. The purpose may be to shift income from the disclaimed property from one to another resulting in income tax savings, or to minimize the estate of the disclaiming beneficiary resulting in estate tax savings. Valuation of estates of the first beneficiaries of the decedent, as well as the estates of persons who might take assets of the decedent's estate as a result of a disclaimer, may be looked to both for income tax and estate tax consequences; and these valuations may be made within the nine months after the death of decedent.

Summary

Valuation, as discussed in this chapter, whether for the purpose of planning, fixing family allowances, determining taxes due or not due, or using the alternate valuation date, is the determination of the market value of property on the proper dates except where special-use valuations are permitted. Valuations may be determined by a variety of methods, depending on the type of property involved, and for tax purposes by application of special tax rules. By proper valuations at the proper times, the desires of the decedent with the maximum benefits to the decedent's beneficiaries can be planned and achieved.

4

How Will My Debts
Be Paid?

In the course of a lifetime every person creates debts. The size and nature of these obligations vary with individual and family situations. It is not surprising that the biggest debts usually are created by the wealthiest people because they have the assets, collateral, and credit rating to support larger borrowings. Unfortunately, many families of average means obligate themselves beyond their abilities to pay, causing financial problems during lifetime and most certainly after death. The biggest obligation is usually the mortgage on the home. In addition, there may be innumerable time payments for cars, appliances, and other items. In any event, these obligations may become a factor to deal with in the administration of an estate.

Take the case of a husband and wife with minor children. If the husband lives to retirement, the mortgage on the home will normally be paid off, along with many other items purchased on credit. But what if the husband dies unexpectedly at an earlier age? He leaves the wife to support the minor children and pay the financial obligations. Further, the main source of income—the husband's earning capacity—is gone. This situation can create quite a hardship on the surviving family members. Therefore, it is the wise man who provides protection for his family in the event of his death.

Provisions in the Will

Most wills specifically provide for the estate to pay debts, taxes, and the cost of administration. Whether or not the will so provides, the personal representative (executor) is under a general duty to pay obligations of the decedent's estate. Will provisions that are unclear may cause confusion, delays, and unnecessary expense. A direction by the testator in a will that "my just debts be paid" is unwise because it may revive debts which would otherwise be unenforceable. It is more appropriate to provide for payment of "my legally enforceable debts."

The phrase "my just debts be paid" may also be interpreted as a requirement for the personal representative to pay off installment debts and long-term mortgage obligations immediately. The careful attorney will avoid this danger by providing that the personal representative shall not be required to pay debts prior to maturity but may extend or renew any debt upon such terms and for such time as he deems best. Thus, the will should explicitly state the intention of the testator. Does he wish the home to pass to the wife burdened with the mortgage or with the mortgage paid, if there are assets to satisfy the mortgage?

Funeral Expenses

Occasionally a testator will include detailed funeral arrangements in his will. If the testator feels strongly about some special funeral arrangements, he should communicate his feelings to some member of the family, because the will is often not readily accessible at the time of death.

Funeral expenses and items incident thereto, such as tombstones, grave markers, crypts, or burial plots, are chargeable against the estate of the decedent. As a matter of public policy, such expenses are granted a high priority for payment. If the testator does not have burial insurance and if he has not otherwise provided for their payment in his will, then funeral expenses will be paid out of such assets as are available in the estate. If prior arrangements have not been made, emotional factors at the time of death can cause excessive funeral expenses.

Estate and Inheritance Taxes

Just as funeral expenses are a kind of involuntary debt against the estate, so are taxes due because of death. The federal and Colorado estate taxes may well be, and in many instances are, the largest costs chargeable to the estate. The reader should carefully review Chapters 6 and 7 for a detailed explanation of this subject.

It is the obligation of the personal representative to pay such taxes as are due. Here again, the testator may have made provisions to satisfy death taxes. If not, then the personal representative must look first to any available cash. If there is none, or if the cash is insufficient, then he must sell securities or other liquid assets to provide the necessary amount. Failure to provide funds for the payment of taxes may destroy the intention of the testator regarding distribution of assets to his beneficiaries.

Many people may not have much cash, but they are wealthy "on paper"—that is, they may own a farm or ranch or other assets that are considerably enhanced in value. The father may wish to leave such assets to his wife or children or both. If, at his death, the size of the estate is such that several thousand dollars in taxes are due, then the only alternative may be to sell all or a portion of the assets to raise the necessary funds.

The situation may arise where the deceased left sufficient assets to pay all the death taxes and other costs but also requested that various specific gifts be made. For example, suppose the home, personal effects, and life insurance proceeds go to the wife, the farm or ranch to the sons, and stocks and bonds to the daughters. Does the testator intend each person bear his or her proportionate share of death taxes, or should the assets be charged against only certain portions of the estate? If insufficient cash is available, which assets should be liquidated first? The will should be clear and explicit with respect to the intention.

Normally testators wish the face amount of the proceeds of life insurance to pass to named beneficiaries in a net amount; thus, it is well to provide in the will that neither taxes nor debts are to be charged against any policies of insurance or the proceeds of such policies.

Planning for the Payment of Debts and Taxes

There are steps that may be taken to minimize probate costs, provide for the payment of debts, and reduce estate and inheritance taxes. A few important suggestions are listed here.

1. A current trust or will, expertly drafted, may clarify many of the problems and, in addition, effect substantial tax savings.
2. A buy-sell agreement for the sale of a business interest at death that is funded with life insurance is usually ideal where the testator is a member of a partnership or a closely held business.
3. A mortgage cancellation policy on the home assures the home's remaining intact.
4. Sufficient life insurance to pay all or some debts, cost of probate, and taxes offsets such costs.
5. Investment in liquid assets that are readily marketable— such as stocks, bonds, and savings—can provide necessary immediate cash.
6. Endowment insurance on the children, designed to mature at the time they are ready for college, will insure future security.
7. Gifts to children or grandchildren, directly or through trusts, give assets to those the testator ultimately wanted to provide for. Gifts may also effect substantial tax savings.
8. A consistent program of saving also insures future security.
9. Careful selection of a personal representative with knowledge, skill, permanency, and financial responsibility is

necessary because of the complicated nature of many estates. Selection of the personal representative may dictate the use of professional help from a bank trust department.

10. Contracting during lifetime for only those obligations that can be paid without financial strain minimizes after-death indebtedness.

11. Consideration of educational, religious, or other charitable institutions as the ultimate beneficiary of the estate is particularly appropriate for a family without children. Even though the survivor may have the benefit of the estate for life, if title rests ultimately in a charity, tax savings may be substantial, since gifts to charity are generally tax free.

Before embarking on any or a combination of these suggestions as part of a formal estate plan, the advice of competent counsel should be sought.

Summary

An unchangeable fact of our existence seems to be death, debts, and taxes. How debts and taxes are paid after death varies in direct proportion to the thought and planning given to them before death. A person who does not avail himself of the wealth of professional estate-planning talent available today is indeed unwise.

There is no substitute for competent legal advice. Home-drawn or do-it-yourself wills usually cause endless litigation and can penalize the family by higher costs and increased taxes. One improper sentence in a will may cause the estate to be improperly taxed, and thus destroy the great advantages that are legally available.

The fee for an attorney to prepare a trust or will which makes proper provision for payment of the debts is small compared to the savings effected and the avoidance of costly delays in probate administration.

5

Time Schedule for Estate Administration

The time necessary to have a will probated or to have an estate administered by the probate court, if there is no will, is often given as a point against permitting an estate to go through probate. Actually, Colorado probate procedure is time consuming only if the particular circumstances warrant it. The federal income and estate tax laws often make it advantageous for the estate to be kept open as long as possible. For example, it could be disadvantageous to close and distribute an estate immediately if having the estate as a separate income taxpayer will divide income between two taxpayers and result in lower income taxes because of taxation at lower rate brackets. Or the estate may need to be kept open to afford time to accumulate funds to pay estate taxes.

Other factors may make a longer period of administration necessary. A poorly planned or drawn will may require a court action before it can be understood. Certain real property title transfers and the handling of certain business interests at death simply cannot be disposed of overnight.

Duties of the Personal Representative

What is involved in Colorado probate and administration? An executor, in Colorado called a personal representative, operating under a simplified procedure, has important duties, some of which must be performed whether or not a living trust has been used by the decedent.

When a Colorado resident dies, the personal representative named in the will sees that burial instructions in the will or in a letter to the personal representative or funeral home are properly carried out even before the will is probated. He looks after unprotected properties such as securities, cash, jewelry, and perishable assets. He determines whether there is adequate insurance against loss. He confers with the heirs, finds out whether the surviving spouse has sufficient funds to meet current living expenses, whether there is a bank or savings account to which the survivor can have interim access, and whether any other problems need immediate attention. He helps with the proof of death for insurance purposes and generally prepares to collect the assets of the estate, which will be his responsibility when the will is probated.

Next, the personal representative must locate the will and have an attorney file it for probate. After being appointed by the court, the personal representative now begins the task of finding out what the estate consists of. He must locate all bank and savings accounts and transfer them to a proper account in the name of the estate. He must identify and determine the terms of all certificates of deposit. He obtains custody of securities, which may or may not be transferred into his name as personal representative, depending on how long the estate will be in administration. He must assume authority over any business owned by the estate, and make arrangements for its management, protection, and continuance so that, if possible, no loss of value or personnel will occur. He must locate and take possession of all other assets of the estate. The personal representative must keep detailed records of all his actions to be sure everything is done properly.

He must not let estate property get mixed with his own property or with the property of any other person. There may be problems with assets that are scattered in different states or even in foreign countries. He must collect all the money owed the estate. He has power to compromise, abandon, or sue for collection of any claim that the estate has and must take appropriate and timely action on all claims.

A detailed inventory of estate assets should be made and either filed with the court or sent to the beneficiaries of the estate. Any interested person can, of course, ask the court to appoint appraisers. The personal representative must estimate how much cash is needed to pay funeral bills, medical bills, and current bills and other debts, as well as taxes and administration expenses. He must provide for any specific cash legacies in the will. If it is necessary to liquidate any assets to provide funds for payment of debts and cash gifts, then the personal representative must see to that. Here he must determine the advisability of sale as opposed to retention of assets for future family use and then arrange and conduct any necessary sales.

He must properly estimate, provide for, and pay the income taxes that will be due for the portion of the year that had elapsed prior to the decedent's death. He must also take care of the estate's income taxes because the estate is a separate income taxpayer, and he must plan for and pay any Colorado and federal estate taxes.

He must collect income as it comes in, and he should watch investments so that appropriate action can be taken to protect estate values. If, for example, the price of a stock held by the estate is going down, perhaps it should be sold in favor of a more promising stock. A proper will provision here makes his task easier.

At the end of the period of administration he must distribute the estate in accordance with the will. He must determine the timing of distributions to beneficiaries with a view toward the most advantageous income tax effect. Here, he must take account of and reconcile as far as reasonably possible any conflicts of interest that arise among the several beneficiaries. If the will calls for the setting up of trusts, he must determine when and to what extent trusts are to be set up, as well as determining which assets should be used to fund the trusts. Handling this properly can mean important tax savings.

After distribution of the estate has been effected and all other disbursements have been properly made, the period of his administration is over.

Time Sequence of Administration

Proving the Will

With this brief outline of the duties of a personal representative, one may more easily understand a timetable of the events of probate. In the typical case, the family makes an effort to locate the will immediately after death in case it contains specific instructions dealing with burial. On rare occasions, the will contains bequests of organs of the body, although a Colorado driver's license notation is much more likely to be effective for that purpose. If there are such instructions, they must be carried out at once. The will is then lodged with the appropriate court.

The total elapsed time to this point may be three or four weeks, depending on how quickly the initial information was assembled. Because most wills are self-proved in Colorado, there is no necessity, even in formal probate proceedings, for the time-consuming process of searching for the witnesses to the will to prove its proper execution. Self-proof provides this necessary element of proving proper execution provided no contention is raised at the time of probate that the testator was incompetent or unduly influenced when the will was made.

Collecting and Valuing Property

Immediately after appointment by the court, the personal representative begins the process of collecting and identifying the assets and determining their respective values. Time involved here depends on the nature and complexity of the estate and the availability and completeness of accounting and other property records. If there are few assets and no claims of consequence, the process of identifying the assets is simple. Valuation for tax purposes may or may not consume an appreciable amount of time, depending on the kind and quantity of the assets involved and whether an appraisal is necessary. If the assets are personal property (household furniture, jewelry, and the like), the period of valuation is relatively short. Essentially, the time element depends on how soon the appraisers can fit an appraisal into their schedules. Usually, only a week or two are involved in this process. Real estate appraisals, on the other hand, generally take longer, partly because the number of persons qualified and available to do real estate appraisals is relatively small, and it takes longer for one of these appraisers to find time to examine the property and make the actual appraisal. The more numerous or sizeable or unique the pieces of real estate, the more time is required for fair and reasonable evaluation.

Understanding the process of real estate appraisal also aids understanding the time requirements. Properties which are similar in type and use to the property owned by the estate will have generally the same characteristics, so the appraiser may arrive at the value of an estate property by considering recent sales of other, comparable properties in the area. Sound evaluation requires that such real estate information be assembled, sorted, and assessed. Although no sale of the estate property is contemplated, it is necessary to establish the fair market value of that property. One must answer a hypothetical question: What would a buyer have been willing to pay a seller who was willing to sell on the date of the decedent's death? While the answer is a matter of opinion, it should have some rational basis that can be documented and made part of the appraisal.

Another kind of property that requires time to value is stock in a closely held corporation. Valuation of listed stock is simple since immediately available market quotations show comparable sales. In contrast, a family corporation in which there may not have been a sale for many years, and in which sales that have occurred may not be representative because of special surrounding circumstances, presents a much more complex problem. A sole proprietorship presents similar problems in locating and identifying sales of similar businesses. Every closely held business is unique, and this uniqueness must be sought out and then, if necessary, demonstrated to the taxing authorities. In all these cases, valuation takes time.

Much time can be saved for a personal representative by a testator's careful preparation for this valuation process. If he leaves a detailed list of assets, accompanied by much of the necessary data for appraisal purposes as well as data showing original cost and the cost of subsequent improvements, his personal representative's job is simplified and shortened.

Paying Creditor Claims

A personal representative moves at his own speed after he has prepared an inventory of the estate. He may take a reasonable time to pay claims against the estate. If the claims are few and uncomplicated, payment can be made rapidly and the estate readied for distribution to the beneficiaries. If litigation arises, or if claims are disputed, the personal representative has adequate opportunity to dispose of these matters in the sensible, normal way that the testator could have done had he lived.

The personal representative may choose to publish a notice to creditors. This must be done in a paper of general circulation in the county of probate. If the decision is made to publish, notice is published once a week for three consecutive weeks. All claims must be presented within four months of the date of first publication or they are forever barred. If a claim is presented, the personal representative can either pay it or disallow it. Since he has 60 days from the end of the creditor's period to deny the claim, it is a good idea to wait for the end of the claim period to review all claims. Any claim disallowed by the personal representative is permanently barred unless a petition for a hearing on the same, or an action against the personal representative is commenced by the creditor within 60 days after the disallowance. If the personal representative does not act on the claim within the permitted period, the claim will be deemed allowed. Consultation with counsel during this period is very critical. If the personal representative decides that no notice is to be published, claims can be filed within one year of the death. In either instance (publication or not), Colorado law prescribes a priority for claims which must be complied with in order to avoid personal liability of the personal representative; again, an attorney should be consulted.

Accounting and Distribution

As soon as taxes and debts have been provided for, the personal representative is ready to make distribution to the beneficiaries under the will. If the administration is not court-supervised (formal probate) and no formal closing is desired, the personal representative has no duty to make any final accounting, unless his actions are challenged by a beneficiary. It is wise to draw up a distribution statement for the information of the beneficiaries and proceed to make a distribution based upon it. Depending on the nature of the assets, the identity and financial circumstances of the beneficiaries, and any resulting conflicts of interest among them, the personal representative will work to reconcile differences and make the most beneficial asset distribution.

Once the asset allocation is determined, actually preparing the distribution statement and making the necessary distribution is essentially a paper-work chore. Where there is no conflict among the beneficiaries and all are aware of the respective interests, such a distribution list may be unnecessary. If adequate accounting records are maintained, they may suffice. However, if a formal closing is used, the personal representative must prepare a formal final account to be filed with the court. Notice must be given to the heirs along with an opportunity to question the account, and a court order must be obtained approving the account and directing the distribution. Then follows the distribution itself, a report to the court that the distribution has been made, and an order from the court approving the report and discharging the personal representative.

Federal Estate Tax

One of the chief reasons for a lengthy probate administration is the nature of the federal tax law.

The federal estate tax return must be filed within nine months after the date of death. This extended period stems from the fact that federal tax law permits an estate to be valued either as of the date of death or as of six months after the date of death, with the personal representative having the option of paying tax at the lower of the two values, an option first granted during the depression of the 1930s. It is desirable, where a federal estate tax may be due and a tax saving is possible, to delay winding up the estate until it can be valued six months from the date of death. Thus, for the protection of the estate, the appraisals mentioned previously have to be made twice—once as of the date of death and again as of six months later. Little, if any, extra time or expense of the appraisers is required for making the second valuation, since most of the work will have been done in the date-of-death appraisal.

The personal representative will usually find it wiser to postpone paying estate tax until it is due, giving the estate the benefit of the use of the money as long as possible. If the estate consists in large part of a closely held business, installment payment of the estate tax is permitted. This allows time for assets to be sold at other than distress prices, and for funds to be accumulated from income to avoid sales of property that should be retained for the family. Timing in these cases, although it involves delay in distribution, works to the benefit of the heirs.

Income Tax

The federal income tax prompts an even longer extension of the administration period. Income tax brackets rise much more sharply than estate tax brackets. For federal income tax purposes, the estate—which comes into being at the moment of death—is a separate taxpayer with a separate exemption and a separate applicable tax bracket. During the period that the estate exists, it provides a separate pocket into which income may be placed and on which federal income tax is payable at a bracket that may be lower than for either the decedent or the beneficiaries. If the tax bracket applicable to the beneficiaries is higher than that applicable to the estate, it will benefit the beneficiaries to maintain the estate as a taxpayer for as long as permissible under federal law.

Estates that remain open from two to five years or more are probably kept open mainly for federal tax reasons rather than delinquency, procrastination, or mismanagement. The simple truth is that a personal representative who does his job thoroughly will not close the estate so long as it is in the best interest of the beneficiaries to keep it open, assuming that he operates within the permissible rules laid down by the Internal Revenue Service and by the courts. The testator's and subsequently the personal representative's planning and judgment will determine whether keeping the estate open for a substantial period is of advantage to the beneficiaries.

6

The Federal Estate Tax

When first enacted in 1916, the federal estate tax affected only families of great wealth. Since that time it has grown in scope until it is often the most formidable claim upon an estate. The federal estate tax affects more and more estates and is a significant factor in estate planning.

The Economic Recovery Tax Act of 1981 (ERTA) has made great changes in the law of federal estate taxation, and those changes will affect future estate planning. With proper planning under ERTA, fewer estates will pay federal estate taxes and significant estate tax deferral will be feasible.

Those alert to the effects of the estate tax take steps during their lives to minimize its impact and make preparation for payment of it. The federal government approves, indeed encourages, proper tax planning, and rewards with substantial savings those who act to minimize the tax. We all face income taxes annually, but estate taxes are faced after death—a time everyone tends to regard as too remote for present consideration. This chapter is written to familiarize the reader with the federal estate tax—the way it will affect an estate and how to prepare for it.

Federal Transfer Tax

To understand how the federal estate tax works, it is necessary to realize that the estate tax is part of an overall federal transfer tax scheme which includes both gift taxes and estate taxes. There is a unified rate of tax for all taxable transfers, whether during a lifetime or at death, and there is a unified credit which makes a certain portion of those taxable transfers exempt from taxation. The unified credit can be used to avoid both gift tax during life and estate tax at death, but to the extent that the unified credit has been used during a lifetime, the amount of credit effectively available at death is reduced.

What Is the Gross Estate?

The federal estate tax is imposed on the transfer of a decedent's property to his beneficiaries. The tax is based on the fair market value of the estate at the time of the decedent's death or, at the option of the taxpayer, on the fair market value of the estate six months after the date of death (the "alternate valuation date"). In addition, there is a special valuation procedure for farm and certain other real property used in a trade or business which may be elected in certain limited circumstances. In a community property state the decedent's estate includes the entire value of all his separate property, as well as his one-half interest in all community property.

The value of the estate for tax purposes includes many things besides the property owned outright by the decedent (such as real property, stocks, bonds, cash and personal effects) at the time of his death. The taxpayer should be aware that the following items may be included in the value of the estate for tax purposes:

1. *Insurance on the decedent's life in which he possessed any "incident of ownership" at the time of his death.* In addition to actual ownership of the policy, an incident of ownership includes the right to change the beneficiary, the right to borrow against the policy, or other similar rights available under an insurance policy.
2. *Property which the decedent conveyed during his lifetime.* Certain gifts made during a lifetime which are in excess of

the annual exclusion amount (that is, gifts which are subject to gift tax) are included as part of the taxable estate. All gifts of life insurance made within three years of death are also included as part of the taxable estate.

3. *Property transferred by owner during his life but in which he retains certain rights.* These rights include the right to use the property for life, to revoke the transfer, to designate who should possess or enjoy the property, or in certain circumstances to vote stock which has been transferred.

4. *The decedent's interest in property owned by him and others as joint tenants with the right of survivorship.*

5. *Certain property which the decedent held the right to direct the disposition of.*

From the foregoing it can be seen that determining what property constitutes a part of the decedent's estate and the value of that property for tax purposes can be complex.

Tax Rates

The federal estate tax is a progressive tax much like the income tax. The rate increases with the value of the estate. Because of the unified credit discussed previously, a certain portion of an estate is exempt from taxation. Table 6-1 shows the exempt portion of an estate and the rate structure for the years 1984 and beyond.

If, for example, an individual dies in 1987, the first $600,000 of his estate will be exempt from taxation. Any excess above that amount will be taxed at an effective rate no lower than 37% and eventually no higher than 50%.

Deductions

Funeral expenses, administration expenses (such as accountant's fees, attorney's fees, costs of property management, and so on), and claims and debts against the estate may be deducted

Table 6-1
Federal Estate Exemption and Rate Structure

Year	Minimum Effective Rate (%)	On Transfers Exceeding ($)*	Maximum Rate (%)	On Transfers Exceeding ($)
1984	34	325,000	55	3,000,000
1985	34	400,000	50	2,500,000
1986	37	500,000	50	2,500,000
1987 or thereafter	37	600,000	50	2,500,000

* Exempt portion of estate.

from the gross estate. What is left is the "net taxable estate." In community property estates the decedent's estate may deduct only half of the community debts and obligations.

In addition, a deduction referred to as the "marital deduction" is allowed for the value of certain property included in the gross estate which passes in a qualifying manner from the decedent to or for the benefit of the surviving spouse. After ERTA, this deduction is unlimited for all property so passing to the surviving spouse. Thus, it is conceivable that federal estate tax may be entirely eliminated in the estate of the first spouse to die if a proper estate plan is used (see Chapter 8). An unlimited deduction is also allowed for the value of all property left to charity.

What Is the Net Taxable Estate?

After the gross estate has been reduced by all deductions (including the marital deduction and any charitable deductions), what remains is the taxable estate. This is the amount against which the tax rates apply.

In determining the tax payable by a decedent's estate, four credits are allowed. A credit is a direct reduction of the tax (as distinguished from a deduction). The most important credit is, of course, the unified credit discussed previously. This credit is available to everyone and determines the exempt portion of the estate, which is shown in Table 6-1. Because of ERTA, the unified credit and the resultant tax-exempt portion of an estate are important in estate tax planning and can be used to reduce overall estate taxes. Other credits include:

1. *State death taxes.* A credit is allowed against the estate tax for the amount of any estate, inheritance, or similar tax paid to any state or the District of Columbia with respect to property included in the gross estate. The amount of this credit is subject to various limitations.
2. *Prior estate taxes paid.* A credit is allowed against the estate tax for any federal estate tax paid on transfer of property to the decedent from a prior decedent (who died within a period up to 10 years before or within 2 years after the present decedent's death). It is not necessary that the transferred property be identified in the present decedent's estate, or that it be in existence at the time of his death. The maximum credit is allowed for 2 years after the prior decedent's death; after that, the credit is reduced by 20% every 2 years. In the third and fourth years, therefore, only 80% of the maximum credit is allowed, and this reduces to 20% in the ninth and tenth year. There is no credit after 10 years.
3. *Foreign death taxes.* A credit is allowed against the estate tax for any estate, inheritance, or similar tax actually paid to a foreign country by the decedent's estate. Again, such credit is subject to various limitations set out in the Internal Revenue Code.

Minimizing the Tax

Proper estate planning minimizes the tax payments. Because of ERTA, it is possible to use both the increased exemption and the unlimited marital deduction to minimize estate tax and to defer that tax until the death of the surviving spouse. Various means can be used to accomplish this goal, one of which includes the creation of trusts which take maximum advantage of the estate tax laws and provide for the descendants of the decedent ultimately to receive the property after the surviving spouse (who has had the benefit of the estate for the rest of his or her life) has died. An example of a tax minimization estate plan for a married couple is one in which the estate is split into two parts. One part is held in trust for the benefit of the surviving spouse and on his or her death is distributed to the children. This trust is funded with assets the value of which equals the exempt portion of the estate in the year of death (see Table 6-1). This trust is technically subject to estate tax, but no tax is incurred since the value of the assets does not exceed the exempt portion of the estate The advantage of this trust is that it is not taxable in the surviving spouse's estate when he or she later dies. It is thus known as a "bypass trust," since it bypasses the surviving spouse's taxable estate and is passed on to the children. The remainder of the estate will pass in such a manner that it qualifies for the marital deduction. Thus, estate taxes can be avoided in the estate of the first spouse to die and maximum use of the unified credit can reduce total tax liability upon the survivor's subsequent death.

Although the use of trusts can frequently help minimize estate taxes, the generation-skipping transfer tax should be considered in planning bypass and other trusts which will be held for the benefit of several generations. The extremely complex provisions of this tax essentially prevent an individual from avoiding estate tax on property passing from generation to generation. At some point, tax on that property will be imposed. There are various exceptions to the generation-skipping transfer tax; however, it remains a factor in estate tax planning.

Paying the Tax

As a general rule, the estate tax must be paid in cash nine months after the date of death. The case requirement and other cash demands upon the estate make it desirable to prepare a proper estimate of the tax liability and proper provisions for payment. "Liquidity" is the term applied to provision for payment of the federal estate tax and other liabilities. Planning liquidity carefully will insure that the estate will not be forced to raise tax funds by selling assets at an unfavorable time or that are difficult to sell. It should be noted that the new unlimited marital deduction which allows for deferral of all taxes until the death of the surviving spouse has to a certain extent removed the liquidity problem in the estate of the first spouse to die.

Under certain circumstances, the personal representative of an estate may obtain an extension of time within which to pay the estate tax. The Internal Revenue Service can allow for "reasonable cause" up to 10 years to pay the tax with interest (the interest rate varies in relation to the prime rate). In addition, a 15-year installment payment plan is available if a specific portion of the estate consists of certain assets such as a closely held business. Under the 15-year payment plan, part of the estate tax bears interest at a rate of 4%. The interest rate on the balance varies in relation to the prime rate. The closely held business exception may apply in certain circumstances where it is not readily apparent, such as ownership of ranches, producing oil leases (working interests), and similar properties which are an active trade or business. The reasonable-cause provision is frequently granted and consent is generally given if a sufficient payment is made on the tax liability equal to the value of the liquid assets of the estate.

Summary

Death and taxes are said to be inevitable. The federal government gives each person an opportunity to plan his estate in a way that minimizes the effect of the federal estate tax. Since the building of an estate is difficult, everyone should become familiar with the provisions of the federal estate tax and prepare for it.

7

The Colorado Estate Tax

For several decades, Colorado had an inheritance tax which was a state death tax system based upon the amount of property received by a beneficiary and the relationship of the beneficiary to the decedent. In 1980, Colorado's inheritance tax was repealed and replaced by the new Colorado estate tax. Under the old inheritance tax, joint safe deposit boxes and joint bank accounts were "frozen" at death and could only be released after approval by the Inheritance Tax Department. This procedure no longer exists.

This new tax (sometimes called a "pick-up tax" or a "gap tax") is applicable only to estates that owe some federal estate tax. It is designed to take advantage of the credit for state death taxes that allows a certain portion of any death tax paid to a state to count as a credit against the federal estate tax. The Colorado estate tax does not cost the estate any additional taxes. If Colorado had no such tax, there would be no credit against the federal estate tax so what would have been a credit must then be paid to the federal government. The Colorado estate tax merely picks up the amount allowed as a credit against the federal tax. This is why the tax is often called a "pick-up tax."

Colorado will claim the maximum credit allowable if the decedent's estate is entirely within this state's jurisdiction. A proportionate share of the credit will be claimed if the decedent dies owning property subject to the jurisdiction of more than one state.

The administration of the Colorado estate tax is under the direction of the Colorado Department of Revenue. This department has broad powers to insure proper enforcement of the tax and may exchange information with the Internal Revenue Service.

A Colorado estate tax return must be filed if a federal tax return is required. The Colorado return must be filed within nine months of the date of death. If the return is not timely filed, there is a penalty equal to 5% of the tax due per month up to a maximum of 25%. However, if an extension to file the federal estate tax return is granted by the Internal Revenue Service, a similar extension will be given for the Colorado return. No penalty is charged during the extension period.

In addition to the penalty for late filing, if the tax is not paid within 9 months of the date of death, it will bear an annual interest until paid at the legal rate set from time to time by Colorado statutes.

8

What Is the Marital Deduction?

"Marital deduction" is an estate tax term that only applies to married couples, and it is a fairly complex subject. However, it can be critically important to people of moderate-to-substantial means. Some of the most helpful "good news" in the Economic Recovery Tax Act of 1981 (ERTA) involves the marital deduction, so a working knowledge of the basic principles is essential.

History of the Marital Deduction

The marital deduction concept is easier to grasp if you know something about its history and how it came to be. The differences between "community property" and "separate property" are discussed in detail in Chapter 16. In a community property state, any property acquired by either spouse during the marriage is considered to be owned by them equally. On the other hand, in a separate property state, assets acquired during marriage by the husband are considered to be his separate property, and property acquired by the wife is considered to be her separate property. In a community property state, even though all of the property has been acquired with the earnings of just one of the spouses, and even though the title to all of the property is in the sole name of that spouse, only one half of the community property is subject to estate tax upon that spouse's death. On the other hand, in a separate property state, if all of the property is acquired from the earnings of one of the spouses, and if the title to the property is in that spouse's name, then the entire value of the property is subject to estate tax in that spouse's estate.

In 1942, Congress undertook to eliminate this tax inequality between community property and separate property states. Its approach was to provide that 100% of community property would be taxed, with certain exceptions, upon the death of the spouse in whose name the property was titled.

That approach created as many problems as it solved, so in 1948 that provision was repealed and the first marital deduction was enacted. Simply stated, that law authorized an estate tax deduction for property passing to a surviving spouse, with a limit equal to one-half the value of the decedent's separate property. Thus, in a common law state the husband could leave up to half of his property to his spouse, take the estate tax marital deduction and achieve the same tax result as a deceased husband in a community property state. For residents of community property states, the marital deduction applied only to a spouse's separate property.

The Tax Reform Act of 1976 modified the estate tax to a "unified transfer tax system," and for the first time the marital deduction could be taken to a limited extent for community property passing to a surviving spouse.

Then, with ERTA came a sweeping change in the form of the "unlimited marital deduction." Now, one spouse may transfer any amount of property, either during life or at death, to the other spouse without tax and *without regard to whether community property or separate property is being transferred.* In tax language we say that there is an unlimited marital deduction for property transferred to a spouse for gift tax purposes on lifetime transfers, and for estate tax purposes on deathtime transfers, emphasizing again that it no longer matters whether the transferred property is separate or community. In fact, for a lifetime gift to a spouse, a gift tax return does not have to be filed, regardless of the value of the gift.

The Marital Deduction and Tax Planning

Now let us address how the marital deduction fits into tax planning for married couples. In how large or how small an estate is it important? May or should trusts be used? Can it be overutilized? When would it be important to use the marital deduction for lifetime gifts?

Unified Credit Coordination

If, after reading about the unlimited marital deduction, the reader jumps to the conclusion that one should simply leave everything to one's spouse and there will be no tax problems, then the importance of coordinating the marital deduction with the unified credit (explained in Chapter 6) will have been overlooked. Depending on the size of the estate, it could be an expensive mistake.

Perhaps a series of simple bar charts will help illustrate how the marital deduction and unified credit should be planned for together, and the dollar values where marital deduction planning becomes important. For simplicity, the illustrations assume all deaths are after 1987 when the exemption equivalent of the unified credit has reached $600,000 and are cast in terms of the husband dying first (since actuarially women outlive men, but the principles are equally important if the wife dies first).

Figure 8-1 assumes a husband and wife each have $300,000 of property for a total family estate of $600,000. Here, the husband's gross estate is $300,000, and his estate tax is zero; however, this zero-tax results from the unified credit without having to use the marital deduction. If he leaves everything to his wife outright (the dashed line indicates the addition to her estate), at her subsequent death her gross estate will be $600,000. Again, the tax will be zero due to the unified credit, and the full value of the family assets will pass to the next generation without any transfer tax. However, remember that this example applies to a decedent who dies in 1987 or later when the unified credit is at its peak.

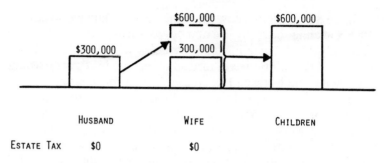

Figure 8-1. Husband and wife with each owning $300,000.

Figure 8-2 assumes a couple of greater means, with each owning $600,000 for a total family estate of $1.2 million in property. This husband's gross estate is $600,000, and again his estate tax will be zero due to the unified credit and regardless of marital deduction. If he leaves his entire estate outright to the wife, her gross estate will be $1.2 million, on which a tax of $235,000 will be owed, thus shrinking the family assets passing to the children to $965,000.

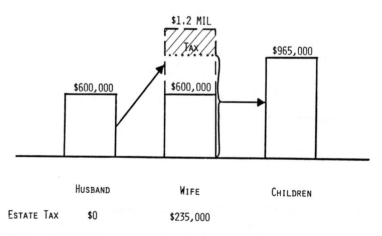

Figure 8-2. Husband and wife with each owning $600,000.

Figure 8-3 illustrates how the same couple could avoid any estate tax at either death by use of a "bypass trust," one of the most frequently used estate-planning vehicles in the past, and one which still has utility. Here, instead of leaving his estate outright to the wife, the husband has created a trust for her; she can receive all of the income during her lifetime and the principal can be used for her support if needed—almost the same financial benefits she would have if the husband left his estate to her outright. But, the trust "bypasses" the wife's estate for tax purposes. Her tax is then zero due to the unified credit, and the full $1.2 million of family assets can be passed to the next generation without any transfer tax.

So far, these hypothetical couples have been able to achieve very attractive tax results without using marital deduction plan-

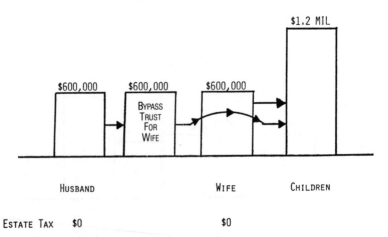

Figure 8-3. Use of the by-pass trust in a husband-and-wife estate of $1,200,000 owned equally.

ning. However, for those with family assets in excess of $1.2 million, where the entire estate belongs to the husband alone, the marital deduction becomes very important. Figure 8-4 assumes a husband with $2 million of separate property. If he leaves it to the wife outright, his estate tax will be zero ($600,000 is exempt from tax under the unified credit, and the excess qualifies for the marital deduction). However, the wife's gross estate will then be $2 million, which will be reduced by a $588,000 estate tax, with a net amount of $1.41 million passing to the children.

Figure 8-5 illustrates how this couple could use a combination of the marital deduction and the unified credit to increase the net amount given to the children by $268,000. Here, the husband places an amount equal to the $600,000 exemption equivalent in a bypass trust for the wife and leaves the excess to her (outright,

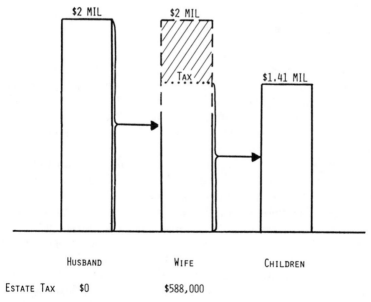

Figure 8-4. Husband with $2,000,000 in separate property.

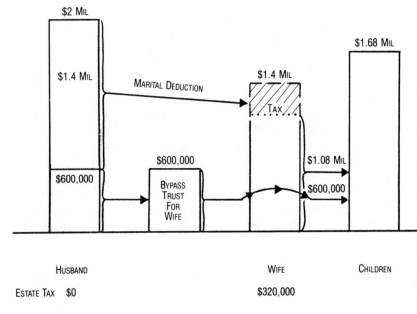

Figure 8-5. Combination of the marital deduction and the unified credit increases the net amount received by children.

for simplicity in this example), thus qualifying for the marital deduction so that his tax is zero. The wife's gross estate, then, is $1.4 million, and her estate tax is only $320,000 (a $268,000 saving) because the husband's estate is not "stacked" on top of hers. Thus, the next generation receives $1.68 million instead of only $1.41 million.

It is important to note that this use of the marital deduction did not completely avoid estate tax on the $400,000 excess over the exemption equivalent in the husband's estate—it simply deferred the tax on that amount until the wife's subsequent death. But tax deferral also means savings, because money which would have otherwise been paid for estate taxes at the husband's death is still available throughout the wife's lifetime, producing income for her benefit. If a 10% annual return were available and the wife survived for 10 years, that would mean a total of $400,000 of additional income for her.

Marital Deduction Trusts

The marital deduction bequest does not have to go to the spouse outright but can be left in trust provided certain requirements are met. Trusts are used basically for three purposes:

1. To provide management of assets.
2. To avoid probate.
3. To save taxes.

A marital deduction trust usually combines all of these objectives.

The one essential ingredient of all marital deduction trust arrangements is that the trust must be structured so that it will be taxable in the surviving spouse's estate; otherwise, a marital deduction will not be allowed in the first spouse's estate.

There are three kinds of marital deduction trusts, the first two of which were used before ERTA and are still workable vehicles in appropriate instances:

1. A marital deduction is allowed for a "power-of-appointment trust" in which (a) the surviving spouse receives all of the income at least annually during lifetime, and (b) has the power (whether exercised or not) to either make unlimited principal withdrawals during lifetime or to specify by will who receives the trust when the surviving spouse dies (which is a "power of appointment" in legal terms).
2. An "estate trust" also qualifies for the marital deduction and differs from the power of appointment trust in that income may be accumulated (and perhaps taxed at a lower bracket) if the trust, including accumulated income, must be distributed to the spouse's estate (and be taxed there) when he or she dies. Sometimes a combination is used where accumulated income must be distributed to a spouse's estate, and the principal is subject to the spouse's power of appointment.

3. ERTA allows a marital deduction for a trust containing "qualified terminable interest property," commonly known by acronym as a "QTIP trust." For the trust to quality: (a) the spouse must receive all of the income at least annually; (b) no one, including the spouse, may have the power to appoint (transfer) the trust property away from the spouse during lifetime; and (c) the executor must make an appropriate election on the estate tax return of the deceased spouse.

The unique feature of a QTIP trust is that the spouse creating the trust may specify who will receive the QTIP property when the surviving spouse dies.

The surviving spouse's estate may recover from the transferees the estate tax paid by virtue of including the QTIP property in the surviving spouse's estate.

Various objectives, such as the desire for management of assets and tax implications, will dictate whether or not to use a marital deduction trust, and if so, what kind. However, since 1981, a larger menu of alternatives is available. Among other things, if a QTIP trust passes to charity after the death of the surviving spouse, it is now possible to avoid any transfer tax at all on the property.

Factors Considered in Marital Deduction Planning

We should ask ourselves whether we should *always* opt for maximum tax deferral by always using the marital deduction to the fullest extent possible.

Assets placed in the bypass trust are sheltered from estate tax at the second spouse's death, and the shelter applies to appreciation in value occurring after the first spouse dies, as well as to the initial value placed in the trust. The alternative to maximum deferral is to pay tax at the first spouse's death (in effect prepay tax which could be deferred by use of the marital deduction) in order to shelter future appreciation from estate tax at the second spouse's death. So, if the family holdings include assets with substantial appreciation potential, full use of the marital deduction might not be the most advantageous result. Furthermore, the taxable income from the family holdings should be considered. In a large estate, if most of the assets are left to the surviving spouse to obtain a maximum marital deduction, he or she will be taxable on all of the income (in a single taxpayer's higher bracket, unless there is a remarriage or head-of-household rates available). If the income is more than the spouse needs, it cannot be shifted without tax consequences to family members in lower tax brackets.

In the past, fairly fixed patterns of marital deduction planning could be established. One basic tenet was that maximum tax results could be achieved if both spouses' taxable estates could be kept approximately equal. But now, in determining to what extent the marital deduction should be used, there are many more variables that cannot be foreseen with precision. The time value of money is an essential part of the equation in comparing the benefits of tax deferral with the benefits of tax-sheltering future appreciation in a bypass trust. On the deferral side, the compound income from the deferred tax can produce high figures, particularly with the high interest rates prevalent over the last few years. In considering the sheltering of future appreciation from tax, compound growth of tax-sheltered assets can be significant, and future taxes should be discounted to present value. The ultimate result of mathematical projections brings life expectancies into play, and people's lives are usually longer or shorter than their actuarial expectancies. So, the reader will find that in the estate-planning process the analysis of his or her own estate will probably be sophisticated, and that in administering an estate important decisions—not always easy ones—will need to be made.

To obtain the marital deduction for a QTIP trust, the executor must elect on the estate tax return for it to apply. One source of flexibility is in the Internal Revenue Code itself, which provides the executor may elect that only a fractional, or percentile, share of the marital deduction bequest shall qualify for the marital deduction. Thus, the will may include different provisions to be applied to the portion of the marital deduction which is not elected, with differing tax consequences, for example, bypass or income-sprinkling provisions, or both. Another alternative provides that if a surviving spouse disclaims all or part of the marital deduction bequest, it will pass in a manner that achieves different tax results, perhaps to a trust sheltered from tax at the second spouse's death, or a trust from which income can be sprinkled to other family members.

Lifetime Gifts

As stated earlier in this chapter, the unlimited marital deduction is available for lifetime gifts to a spouse. While there are not now as many tax-motivated reasons for lifetime giving between spouses due to the fact the tax can be reduced to zero at the first death, there is still much more freedom to make such gifts for whatever reasons—other than taxes—a spouse may want to.

One instance where tax planning could motivate a lifetime gift from spouse to spouse is where one spouse has substantially more property than the other plus a longer life expectancy. Figure 8-6 shows a husband with a $300,000 gross estate, and a wife several years younger than he, who, because of an inheritance, has a gross estate of $900,000 (on which there will be an estate tax of $114,000 at her death). If the wife makes a $300,000 lifetime gift to the husband, his gross estate becomes $600,000, on which there will be no tax due to the unified credit. He could leave it to a bypass trust for the wife so that her gross estate is reduced to $600,000 by the lifetime gift, and the entire family assets of $1.2 million can be passed to the children tax-free under the unified credit. The result is the same as in Figure 8-3, where the spouses had equal estates.

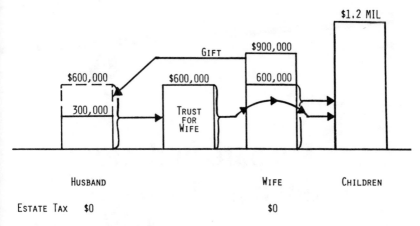

Figure 8-6. A lifetime gift from spouse to spouse can result in tax savings.

Summary

This chapter covers an extensive subject in summary form and contains some oversimplification of the complexities experienced in estate planning for the marital deduction or during the administration of an estate. However, a basic understanding of the fundamentals of the marital deduction is important in the planning of estates of married couples.

9

Probate and Tax Savings Through Gifts

Gift giving often plays a part in passing property from one generation to the next, even without the motivation of estate planning. Parents may transfer an interest in the family business to their children in order to increase the children's interest in the enterprise and to equip them to assume the responsibilities of management. Farmers and ranchers often give their children a few head of livestock so that they may acquire experience in animal husbandry or have an opportunity to build a herd of their own over the years. Husbands often place securities in trust to assure income for their wives. Parents may do the same for the protection of their children.

In addition, gifts often have the benefit of reducing income and estate taxes, as well as lowering the costs of probate. In planning gifts, however, the welfare of the person making the gift and the welfare of the one receiving it should be the paramount considerations. An older person should not make gifts that would impair his security, his capacity to provide for himself, or his opportunity to continue useful and gainful employment. A child should not be given funds or property which he is too young to handle. The selection and timing of gifts to young people who lack experience in financial mangement should be designed to further their proper training and development, with adequate provisions for the care and management of property. A desire to effect a tax savings or to avoid probate costs should be secondary considerations when compared with the value of the property involved. It is better to provide for the payment of taxes and other costs by additional life insurance or some other method than to make gifts which would prejudice the security of the giver or be unsuited to the position of the receiver.

Gifts Save Taxes

Prior to 1977, substantial tax savings could be gained by passing property from one generation to the next by making lifetime gifts rather than by simply letting the property pass through the estate at the time of death. If a person made gifts to his descendants, the property would usually be out of his taxable estate. The gift tax on such gifts was generally significantly lower than the estate tax which would have resulted had no gift been made. The Tax Reform Act of 1976, however, eliminated the bonus of lower gift tax brackets as a tax incentive for major gift giving, and the Economic Recovery Tax Act of 1981 (ERTA) continues the unified rate schedule format. Now, for purposes of determining the size of a person's taxable estate at-death most gifts will be treated as if they had never been made, while any gift tax paid on a lifetime gift will be credited against the estate tax due. Nevertheless, although the major tax advantage of gift giving, the lower tax brackets, has been eliminated, there are still some significant tax advantages to be obtained by lifetime gift giving.

Giving Appreciating Assets

One tax advantage to lifetime gift giving is that, although generally the value of a gift made during the donor's life will be included in determining the size of his total taxable estate upon his death, if the item has appreciated in value between the time the gift was made and the time the donor died, then that appreciation will not be included in the estate. For example, if a parent were to give to his children land worth $100,000 at the time the gift was made, but over the years the land appreciated in value so that when the parent died the land was worth $150,000, then only $100,000 would be reincluded in his taxable estate and the $50,000 of appreciated value would escape taxation. If the gift had not been made then the entire $150,000 worth of land would have been included in the parents' taxable estate. Thus, giving away assets likely to appreciate in value over the years still has tax advantages.

The other side of the coin, however, is that the taxpayer should avoid giving away property likely to decrease in value over the years, because the value of the property at the date of gift will be included in the donor's estate no matter what the value of the property at the date of his death. If the property in the preceding example had decreased in value to $50,000, then the $100,000 value would still be included in the taxable estate, whereas if the gift had not been made, then only $50,000 worth of property would have been included in the taxable estate. This will make for an extremely unhappy taxpayer.

Removal of Gift Taxes

A second tax advantage of lifetime gift giving is that the money used to pay gift tax is not included in the donor's estate when he dies. Going back to our preceding example, if the parent had paid a $30,000 gift tax on the gift of $100,000 worth of land, then that $30,000 would not be left to be taxed when he died. However, under the new law where that $100,000 gift must be reincluded in the taxable estate, the $30,000 of gift tax paid will be credited against the estate tax due and, therefore, the taxpayer is using tax free dollars to pay his estate tax. If no gift had been made, then the $30,000 which would have been used to pay a gift tax would be left in his taxable estate and subject to estate tax. At the time this book was being prepared, the Treasury Department was considering legislation to eliminate this advantage.

Contemplation-of-Death Gifts

If the donor dies within three years of the date of the gift, special rules affect the advantages discussed previously. Prior to 1982, the rule was that any gift made within three years of death was included in the donor's estate and, in addition, the gift tax paid on the subject gift was reincluded in the estate. This means that the gift, including appreciation and the amount used to pay the gift tax, would not escape estate taxation if death occurred within three years of the gift.

ERTA provides a new rule for estates of decedents dying after 1981. With certain exceptions, the three-year rule will not apply to those estates, and post-gift appreciation will not be subject to transfer tax. Therefore, under the new rules, a taxpayer can literally give away $10,000 to each of an unlimited number of family members and relatives on his deathbed without gift or estate tax consequences. The major exception to this rule concerns gifts of life insurance policies within three years of the donor's death. It is still the rule that gift taxes paid on gifts within three years of death are included in the donor's estate.

Gift Tax Annual Exclusion

A third way that gift giving can save estate taxes is with the annual exclusion. ERTA raised the annual exclusion amount from $3,000 to $10,000 effective for gifts made after 1981. Each person may now make gifts of up to $10,000 a year to any number of people tax free. Moreover, such annual exclusion gifts will not be reincluded in the donor's estate at death. Thus, all such gifts will escape both gift and estate taxation. The provision for an annual exclusion was originally included to permit normal periodic gifts such as wedding and Christmas presents among family members and friends without the discouraging effect of taxes. The exclusion is $10,000 *per donee*, so the amount that can be given away, tax free, under this provision is limited only by the number of persons to whom gifts are made. For example a man with four children could make gifts to the next generation of up to $40,000 a year tax free. If he were joined by his wife who agreed to combine her exclusion with his, then together they could give away $80,000 a year to their children tax free. As you can see, if a husband and wife were to establish such a gift giving program, then over a period of 10 years they could divest themselves, tax free, of the quite substantial sum of $800,000 worth of property. The power of a husband and wife to combine their exclusions applies even though the property given might be the separate property of either spouse. Such annual exclusion-giving programs can be very attractive.

To qualify for the annual exclusion, gifts must be made in a manner which gives the recipient immediate access to the gift. Thus, with a few exceptions, most gifts intended to qualify for the annual exclusion must be made outright or to custodians and cannot be made in trust.

An important exception to this rule is that the annual exclusion may be used when a gift is made in trust for a child, if the trust terminates when the child reaches age 21 and if the trust contains certain other provisions required by the Internal Revenue Code. These provisions include a requirement that distributions of income and principal be made only to or for the benefit of the child. Such trusts may be included in the estate of the donor for estate tax purposes if the donor serves as trustee, unless carefully drafted from a legal standpoint. Such an arrangement works well when a grandparent desires to make a gift in trust to a grandchild and appoints his child as the trustee.

A second exception is that the annual exclusion may also be used when gifts are made to a trust that can be revoked by the beneficiary. For tax purposes such gifts are considered equivalent to outright gifts to the beneficiary. A competent legal advisor can devise a trust that may extend well past the age of 21 as a practical matter, although legally the beneficiary has the right to terminate the trust at age 21.

Gift Tax Credit

A fourth factor to keep in mind in evaluating the tax advantages of gift giving is the unified system of tax credits. ERTA provides up to $192,800 in tax credits that can be applied against the gift tax during a person's lifetime. (The new law provides for a gradual increase in the tax credit from $62,800 in 1982 to a maximum of $192,800 in 1987.) Because a gift of around $600,000 will incur a tax of about $192,800, a taxpayer living until 1987 will be able to give away as much as $600,000 during his life without paying a tax at the time the gifts are made.

Of course, the tax will come at the time of death when the gifts are reincluded in the taxable estate. This still provides a significant benefit, if a person desires to give away property that is worth less than $600,000 at the time of the gift but is expected to rapidly appreciate. Remembering the case of the parent who gave away land worth $100,000 at the time of the gift but worth $150,000 at the time of his death, you can see that he could obtain the benefit of removing $50,000 worth of appreciation from his taxable estate without any transfer tax cost.

Income Tax Savings From Giving

Another tax advantage of lifetime gifts that must be considered is the income tax savings that may result from transferring income producing property from a high bracket taxpayer to a low bracket taxpayer. If a parent were a 50 percent bracket income taxpayer and his child were a 20 percent bracket income taxpayer, then a gift of property that produced a $5,000 a year income would result in a $15,000 income tax savings to the family over a period of 10 years. If the parent had kept the gift he would have had $50,000 of income and paid $25,000 in income tax. But after the gift, the child will pay only $10,000 in income tax on the same $50,000 income. Often the income tax savings alone prompts such gifts.

A common device to accomplish this shifting of income but yet retaining the right to get the principal back after a period of time is a short-term trust commonly known as the Clifford Trust. Generally, it requires the principal to be left in trust for at least 10 years before it can terminate. This device is quite successful in financing children's college educations or providing for the support of elderly parents who need help, because it shifts income to the lower tax brackets of the people who are going to get the money anyway, yet the principal is not given away permanently.

As an added bonus, any income produced from gift property will not be included in the donor's taxable estate. If the parent with property producing income of $5,000 a year transferred it to a trust for a child 10 years before the parent's death, then $50,000 (less income taxes), which would have been in the parent's taxable estate had he kept the property, would not be in the parent's taxable estate.

How Gift Tax Is Figured

When gifts to a single person exceed the $10,000 annual exclusion, a gift tax return must be filed. The gift tax is computed on a cumulative basis. When taxable gifts are made, the amount of the tax is determined by calculating the gift tax due on an amount equal to all past and current gifts and subtracting from it the tax that would be due on all past gifts. For this reason, gift tax brackets increase as taxable gifts are made. For example, if in 1982 a single person with no prior gifts makes a gift of $50,000 to one person, then he has made a gift subject to taxation in the amount of $40,000 ($50,000 less the $10,000 annual exclusion). The gift tax on such an amount is $8,200. If he made a similar gift of $50,000 the next year, his gift tax would be calculated as follows:

Total taxable gifts made to that date	$80,000
Gift tax on $80,000 taxable gift	$18,200
Less gift tax on $40,000 taxable gift	8,200
Gift tax on the gift in the second year	$10,000

Note that the first year's gift was taxed at a top bracket of 22 percent but the second year's gift was taxed at a top bracket of 26 percent. Of course, no tax would actually have been paid in either year because the taxpayer would use $8,200 of his tax credits the first year and an additional $10,000 of credit the next year.

The tax on the same amount of gifts made by a married couple instead of a single person will be roughly half, because of the married couple's ability to split their gifts.

Techniques for Making Gifts

Because the best interests of the family members or other beneficiaries of the trust should be the paramount consideration, it is often best to incorporate into a trust those provisions that provide the best family scheme, even if it requires the payment of some tax. Each individual should weigh with his counselor the tax benefit against the amount of control the donor must give up to obtain that tax benefit.

Custodial Gifts to Minors

If gifts are made to a minor, a guardian or conservator may be appointed by the court to administer the estate of the recipient. In Colorado, a guardian is primarily the person designated to have physical custody of a minor child or incompetent adult. This person makes decisions regarding the welfare of the designated minor child or incompetent adult. A conservator is the person given the authority to handle the property of a minor or incompetent person and makes decisions relating to investments and the management of all types of assets which the protected person owns or may be entitled to receive. Statutes have been enacted under which certain gifts may be made to a "custodian" who holds the property for a minor. In addition, there are various types of trusts which are commonly used.

Gifts which come under the administration of conservators often result in legal problems and therefore may not be desirable. Conservatorship laws are designed to provide the maximum protection for the protected person. Annual court accountings are required. In addition, unless the conservator is a bank or trust company, the conservator must post a surety bond and is severely restricted in investing his ward's funds. These and other provisions may occasion expense and complications. Thus, the management of property by conservators tends to be inflexible, cumbersome, and expensive as well.

Custodial arrangements were created by statute as a simplified means of allowing an adult to hold and manage property for a minor. The custodian does not have to post a bond and the procedure for establishing a custodial arrangement is very simple. A person desiring to make a gift under the custodianship provisions simply makes the gift to "John Doe as custodian for Bobby Doe under the Colorado Uniform Transfers to Minors Act." In recent years, the powers of a custodian have been enlarged to allow investments in securities, real property, tangible personal property, life insurance, and, of course, money. The custodianship, however, is still less flexible than a trust arrangement because it is automatically dissolved when the child reaches the age of 21, whereas a trust can terminate at any age stipulated in the trust instrument. Also, under a custodianship, if the child dies before reaching the age of 21, all of the property must go to his estate. This is not required in a trust agreement, for the trust instrument may stipulate exactly to whom the property is to go if the child dies before the trust is terminated.

During the term of the custodianship, the custodian has complete freedom to sell the property and reinvest the proceeds in permissible investments. He has complete discretion on how the property will be used subject to the limitation that it must be used for the benefit of the minor.

The income from the custodial property is taxed to the minor. This usually results in tax savings since the minor will be in a lower income tax bracket. Although transfers to a custodian represent completed gifts for gift tax purposes, when a person names *himself* custodian for his own minor child, as in the case of a father for his son, the gift will be included in the taxable estate of the father if he dies before his son reaches 21. Therefore, it is usually best to name someone other than the person making the gift as the custodian. This might be the spouse, a grandparent, or some other adult.

Gifts in Trust

For hundreds of years the gift in trust has been the accepted method of making gifts where an outright gift is inappropriate. In almost every case this method is preferable to a gift to a guardian or conservator, and it is generally more flexible than a custodianship. In a trust the giver can specify the rules he desires applied to the management of the property given and to the use of the property by the beneficiary. The terms of the trust may be more or less stringent than a custodianship or conservatorship, and provisions may be inserted for many eventualities. The preparation of a trust requires the services of a lawyer, but the cost of these services ordinarily will be a small fraction of the value of the property involved and the income it produces. An individual may serve as a trustee. If a bank or trust company serves as the trustee, the fees normally will be no higher than in the case of comparable services from a conservator, guardian or custodian. The legal expenses involved in the establishment and operation of a trust should be materially less than those involved in a conservatorship or guardianship covering the same amount of property. In any individual case, however, the alternative advantages and disadvantages of various modes of making gifts will involve legal issues on which competent advice can be obtained only from a professional who is familiar with trust matters.

If property or appreciation in property given in trust is to be removed from the estate of the donor for estate tax purposes, the gift must be irrevocable, and the donor must part with the right to receive income from it. Furthermore, the donor must forego the right to determine how trust benefits will be shared among the beneficiaries. This may be accomplished in a trust of which the donor is trustee. However, it is usually desirable to utilize an independent trustee where gifts in trust are made by a living person and estate tax considerations are important. The variations in arrangements that will meet the various tax requirements are numerous, and the controlling rules are technical and complex. Therefore, the lawyer who drafts such instruments must develop a recommendation in each case that will comply with such rules while fulfilling family needs.

Bargain Sale

A variety of more specialized devices may be considered in larger estates where estate tax problems are especially critical. It may be helpful to combine a gift with a sale of property to one's children by selling property that will appreciate in value. The seller will ordinarily realize no immediate taxable gain from such a sale, and the amount of the gift will be the difference between the property value and the sales price. Property may be sold to children or others for its actual value with the purchase price payable in installments. The payment of the installments may be forgiven or cancelled as they become due. This approach may be more practical where there has been no substantial appreciation in the property's value since it was acquired by the seller.

Irrevocable Life Insurance Trusts

Special types of gifts may be desirable to permit a spouse or child to carry insurance on the life of the working spouse. Such gifts may enable the family to keep the insurance proceeds out of the taxable estate at the breadwinner's death and yet have liquid funds available for payment of taxes or for other needs. Properly structured, such trusts may also provide lifetime income and other benefits to the surviving noninsured spouse while keeping the remaining proceeds out of such surviving spouse's taxable estate at death. Trusts for the purpose of owning such insurance are subject to special provisions of the tax laws and must be separately considered.

Family Business Organizations

Where larger amounts of property are involved, other types of special arrangements may be required. It may be desirable to change the form of organization of the parents' business to create interests that are easily transferred by gift. For example, voting rights and other factors affecting stock in a family enterprise may be modified so that shares are created that are appropriate for gift purposes. In such circumstances, special consideration must be given to the effect that such stock provisions may have on the valuation of the shares. In other cases, a family limited partnership might be desirable. The parents could be the general partners and the children the limited partners, allowing centralized management of family properties but relative ease in transferring ownership interests. Each situation presents different problems and there is no ready-made solution for all. For this reason the development of an appropriate solution in an individual case should take into consideration the economic and tax positions of the parties, the proper management of the property, and above all the best interests of the persons involved. A detailed discussion of the planning opportunities in family businesses is in Chapter 21.

10

Should I Make Gifts to Charity?

Charitable donations have become an accepted and sometimes expected part of today's society. Individual contributions, compared to corporate or foundation grants, compose almost 90% of the $53 billion raised for philanthropy in 1981. The decision to make gifts to charity, either during one's lifetime or by will, is a personal matter. Obviously, the selection of the charity, the timing, the amount, and the type of property given will depend upon the individual's attitude, desires, financial resources, and responsibilities.

Once the decision has been made to contribute to charity, or at least to consider it, the tax effects of the gift become important; income, gift, and estate tax deductions are allowable for certain charitable gifts. Often, income taxes are the largest item of an individual's budget, and in many instances, the estate tax bill is the largest expense of the deceased's estate. If a person can accomplish his charitable objectives and reduce his tax bill, he is apt to be a "cheerful giver."

Gifts of Cash or Property

When considering some sort of charitable contribution by will, most people think in terms of a cash bequest of a fixed amount with the bulk of the estate passing to the surviving family. Under such circumstances the entire amount of the charitable bequest is usually deductible for federal estate tax purposes.

Often, however, cash will be needed in the estate to defray costs of administration and taxes. Payment of the charitable legacies in cash could produce a cash shortage, necessitating the sale of other properties. The estate may be composed primarily of real estate or closely held corporate stocks, which may be non-liquid in the sense that they cannot be sold easily. Sale of those properties either to pay the charitable cash bequest or to restore the cash used to pay the charity may not only be inconvenient but may result in an income tax if the property sold has appreciated in value between the date of the decedent's death and the time of the sale. To avoid these problems, the individual may wish to leave property to charity in his will instead of cash. The entire value of the property given will usually be estate tax deductible.

Fixed Amount or Percentage

Instead of giving a specific dollar amount or designated properties to charity, one may wish to consider giving a fixed percentage of his estate. If the will is drafted so that administrative costs of the estate do not come out of the gift, the entire gift will be deductible for federal estate tax purposes. Another advantage of the percentage gift is an across-the-board reduction of the gift if the estate has a lower value than the donor expected.

Trust Gifts

Family responsibilities may prevent a substantial outright gift by will to charity. However, family circumstances may make it possible to make a charitable gift in trust of the income or of the remainder in certain properties. For example, a person may wish to provide a life income to his spouse or to his parents with the property ultimately passing to charity. Or he may feel that adequate provision has been made for his children during their minority and arrange for the income from the property to be paid to charity until the children become adults at which time they will receive the property.

Under either arrangement the present value of the charity's income interest or remainder interest would be deductible for estate tax purposes if the trust included a number of safeguards in order for the charity's interest to be well defined. In our example where the spouse or parents received income for life, the trust could be a *charitable remainder unitrust* or a *charitable remainder annuity trust*. In our example where the charity received the income until the children were adults, the trust would be a *charitable lead trust*. The elimination of all estate tax while satisfying family and charitable objectives is not uncommon and should be discussed with counsel.

Lifetime Gifts

If a person has decided to make charitable contributions, it may be appropriate to consider making them while still living. Lifetime outright gifts and any subsequent appreciation in their value, of course, are eliminated from the donor's estate. Their values are completely deductible for gift tax purposes, and unlike most charitable gifts made by will, lifetime gifts to charities may result in an income tax deduction to the donor.

For example, if a person wishes to give certain property to charity at his death, it may be desirable for him to establish a trust during his lifetime, reserving an income interest for himself for life with the remainder going to charity at his death. Since the only gift is that of the remainder interest and it is given to charity, there would be no gift tax. The value of the property in the trust has not been removed from the donor's estate for estate tax purposes because the income was reserved for life. However, since the property will pass to charity at his death, it will be deductible from the gross estate. Moreover, the value of the remainder interest given to charity is deductible for income tax purposes providing safeguards for defining the charity's interest are included in the form of a charitable remainder annuity trust or unitrust.

The amount of the income tax deduction varies with the length of time the charity must wait for the gift, but the deduction is immediate so that spendable dollars in the year of the gift are increased. The income interest is paid to the donor for the rest of his life.

Under such arrangement properties which have appreciated in value since the donor acquired them may be given to the trust. It is better to contribute these appreciated properties to the trust and obtain a higher income tax charitable deduction than to sell the properties, pay the capital gain tax and contribute the remaining proceeds to the trust.

Income Tax Deduction for Gifts

There are limitations on the amount of charitable gifts that are tax deductible within a given year. Generally, charitable contributions to public charities are deductible up to 50% of the contribution base, which is adjusted gross income subject to certain adjustments. Contributions to certain charitable foundations, on the other hand, are deductible up to only 20% of the contribution base. The size of the charitable contribution in any particular year must be carefully planned if all of it is to be tax deductible. The excess of a charitable donation to a public charity over the income tax limitations can be deducted in the five following years. Alternatively, the donations can be made over a period of years. Thus, rather than giving a block of stock in one particular year, a smaller number of shares might be given over several years. Similarly, undivided interests in real estate can be given periodically to maximize available income tax benefits.

Gifts of Life Insurance

There are, of course, other methods of making charitable contributions. One of these involves using life insurance. An individual may transfer to charity an existing life insurance policy and be entitled to a charitable deduction based on the value of the policy. Subsequent premium payments will also be deductible for income tax purposes. If the donor keeps the policy but names the charity beneficiary, the proceeds are includable in his estate but deductible as an estate tax charitable deduction.

Charitable Foundations

If the donor wishes to make substantial gifts to charity, he might consider establishing his own charitable foundation. Usually an individual establishes a foundation in the form of a non-profit corporation. A ruling is obtained from the Internal Revenue Service. Subsequent gifts to the foundation are deductible for income, gift, and estate tax purposes, and the income of the foundation, with certain restrictions, is tax free.

The individual or his family usually controls the investment and donation policies of the foundation. The foundation makes investments which are almost entirely tax free and also makes grants to other charities. The individuals can thereby maximize their potential for charitable giving. Their foundation will memorialize their name as well as any cause they may be supporting. It can introduce their children to the importance their parents place on charitable giving. Charitable foundations are subject to complex rules and restrictions so care must be exercised in their creation and operation in order to maintain the exemption from tax.

Because of suspected widespread abuse with some private foundations, Congress in 1969 imposed substantial limitations upon the activities of private foundations. Because of the complexity of complying with the new limitations, the establishment of small private foundations has sharply declined in recent years. Nevertheless, despite these complexities, the establishment of a private foundation which is properly organized and operated may still be advantageous.

Gift of Remainder Interest in
Personal Residence

A donor may wish to contribute the remainder interest in his personal residence, farm, vacation home, or stock in a cooperative apartment used as a residence. The donor retains the right to live in his residence or use it for a term of years or for the rest of his life and the life of his spouse. The donor is entitled to an immediate income tax deduction based on the value of the remainder interest in the residence contributed to charity.

Pooled Income Funds

These are similar in concept to mutual funds. They are offered by many charities in Colorado. A donor contributes generally cash or securities to the fund and receives his pro rata share of the fund's income for the rest of his life. Upon his death his share of the fund is then given to the charity. He not only receives an immediate charitable income tax deduction but also avoids any tax on the appreciation in any securities contributed. The fund managers diversify the fund's investments and maximize the return. A pooled income fund permits a donor with highly appreciated but low yielding stock to diversify and increase his income while paying no tax on the capital gain and receiving a current income tax deduction.

Gift Annuities

Many charities are licensed in Colorado to sell gift annuities. The donor transfers money or property to the charity in exchange for the annuity. He receives a guaranteed fixed sum usually monthly, commencing either immediately or at a future date and continuing for the rest of his life and the life of his spouse. The donor receives a charitable income tax deduction and favored treatment on any capital gain in the property transferred to the charity.

Summary

The manner in which charitable gifts can be most advantageously utilized by the individual depends on the amount and nature of his assets and the relationship of the income, gift, and estate taxes to his own particular situation. Apart from tax advantages, charitable giving often makes good sense for family reasons. Coordination of charitable contributions with plans for individual or family estate planning often results in maximizing one's charitable and personal objectives.

11

Should I Make a Will?

Most people work hard to acquire and keep property during their lifetimes. However, a surprisingly large number of people die without a will. Those people forfeit the right to determine the disposition of their property and fail to provide for their family's continued well-being. They die leaving the security of their family to chance and the disposition of their property to the law.

Who Can and Should Make a Will

The records of the probate courts in Colorado show that wealthy people usually recognize the value of planning their estate. Most of the persons who die without a will are the owners of modest or medium-sized estates. Yet, saving a dollar in a small estate means much more to that family than saving a dollar would to a family with a $1 million estate.

A will is a written instrument by which a person (called a testator) disposes of his property effective at his death. It is always subject to change by the maker during his lifetime. It conveys no present interest in property or rights to any beneficiary until the maker's death. As a result, a will can dispose of property acquired after the will was made.

Colorado law gives to every person of sound mind who is at least 18 years old the right to make a will. This right carries with it the privilege of disposing of one's estate in any manner and to anyone. Colorado law does not require that property be left to one's children, parents, or any other person. However, a spouse may not be disinherited unless such spouse has signed a valid waiver of his or her marital property rights. In the absence of such an agreement, the disinherited spouse may elect to take against the will and receive one half of the "augmented estate" of the deceased spouse. This includes the probate estate plus certain lifetime transfers.

Types of Wills

There are basically two types of wills provided for by Colorado law. The most common type is the typewritten will, usually prepared by an attorney. For such a will to be valid it must be in writing and signed by the maker (testator) or by someone signing for him at his direction and in his presence. This form of will must be attested by two competent witnesses who must also sign their names to the will in their own handwriting and in the presence of the person making the will. In Colorado, unlike many other states, a witness may be a beneficiary under the will.

If the requirements for execution of the will and its attestation are not strictly complied with, the will is invalid and may be contested. Likewise, if the maker is not of sound mind or is acting under undue influence when the will is executed, it is invalid. Hence, it is advisable to have an attorney supervise the making and execution of a will to make certain all of the prerequisites for validity and the various formalities of execution have been satisfied.

A "self-proved will" is one in which the signatures of the testator and witnesses are notarized, in addition to the other formal requirements for valid execution. This feature allows the will to be admitted to probate at the death of the testator in a formal probate proceeding without the testimony of the witnesses. A will is not invalid if it does not have this self-proving feature.

The other type of will valid in Colorado is one in which the signature and the material provisions are written wholly in the handwriting of and signed by the testator. This is a "holographic" will and does not require witnesses in order to be valid. A typewritten instrument, or one written by someone other than the maker, is not a holographic will and must be properly executed and witnessed.

Dying Without a Will

When a person dies in Colorado without a will, the laws of intestate succession determine who shall inherit his property and in what proportions the property shall be distributed. These laws also govern the distribution of property not disposed of by a decedent's will, either because the will does not cover all of the property or because it is invalid. Where there is a will, unless a contrary intention is plainly expressed or necessarily implied, it will be presumed that the maker intended to dispose of his entire estate according to its terms.

The properties disposed by a decedent's will, or by the laws of intestate succession, are only the decedent's separate property and his half interest in any community property. His will has no effect on property owned with another person in joint tenancy. Upon the death of a joint tenant, the property passes to the survivor by operation of law regardless of the provisions in the decedent's will or the laws of intestate succession. The will also has no effect on life insurance payable to a named beneficiary or on property in a revocable living trust.

Table 11-1 shows how property not disposed of by a will is distributed to the heirs at law in Colorado.

This illustrated distribution of property is the will which the State of Colorado has written for a person who does not take the opportunity to make his own. It is inflexible and does not take into account the individual needs and requirements of the various family members.

If a father dies without a will, his wife receives roughly only one half of the estate, an exempt personal property allowance of

Table 11-1
Property Distribution Without a Will

Decedent Survived By:	With No Will, Property Goes To:				
	Spouse	Decedent's Children and Descendants	Decedent's Parents	Decedent's Brothers, Sisters and Their Descendants	Decedent's Grandparents and Their Descendant
Spouse No children or descendants	All				
Spouse Children or descendants of both decedent and surviving spouse	First $25,000 plus one-half balance	One half of everything exceeding first $25,000			
Spouse Some children or descendants not by surviving spouse	One half	One half			
No spouse Children or descendants		All			
No spouse No children or descendants But parents			All		
No spouse No children or descendants No parents But brothers or sisters				All	
No spouse No children or descendants No parents No siblings or their descendants					All

$7,500, and a 12-month allowance for support. If these amounts are not sufficient to support her, she will have to go to work or find other means of support since the balance of the property belongs to the children and cannot be used for the wife's support unless the children are adults and choose to make gifts to the wife for this purpose. This is hardly the disposition the owner of a modest or medium-sized estate wants in order to protect the best interests of his wife and children. Yet, this is his will, unless he does something about it.

When a parent is survived by minor children, the problems presented by dying without a will are particularly acute. The surviving spouse is obligated to support the children, and often is required to do so out of his or her own property and earnings, even though the children may have substantial inheritances of their own. Where a minor receives property through inheritance, it is often necessary to have a conservator appointed, not only to protect the property and the minor's rights, but also because the law may require a conservator before a distribution can be made. Insurance companies and governmental agencies, such as the Social Security Administration and the Veterans Administration, may require a conservatorship before they will pay funds to a minor beneficiary. Where a minor inherits an interest in real estate, title companies and lending agencies may require that a conservatorship be established before the minor's interest can be sold.

The complications are potentially even greater when an unmarried person without children dies intestate. The Colorado statute then distributes the estate to the closest living blood relative. In some cases, this may be a remote cousin who is relatively a stranger to the decedent. Figure 11-1 shows the degrees of relationship between a decedent and those who may take his estate.

Conservatorship—Penalty of Dying Without a Will

The administration of the minor's property under a conservatorship is highly restricted, costly, and subject to court supervi-

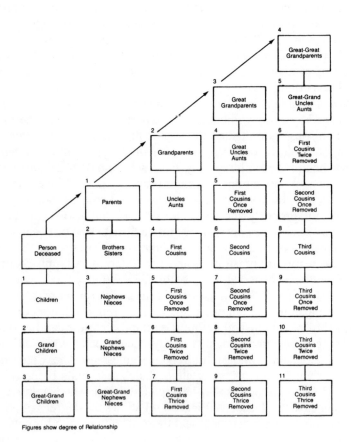

Figures show degree of Relationship

Figure 11-1. Degrees of Relationship.

sion to safeguard the minor's rights. The minor's money can be invested only in authorized investments, and the conservator's expenditures are also regulated. The court may insist that the conservator post a bond, with sureties as it may specify, conditioned upon the faithful discharge of the conservator's duties, all at the expense of the minor's estate. Additionally, the conservator is entitled to reasonable compensation from the estate with court approval.

When the minor reaches age eighteen, the conservator must deliver the minor's property to him regardless of the maturity or business experience of the minor. The minor is entitled to a full accounting from the conservator as to the handling of the minor's property during the entire period of the conservatorship, and should the minor be displeased with the results of the accounting, litigation may follow.

One of the unique advantages of making a will is the opportunity for the parent or grandparent to establish a trust to administer the minor's property. Such a trust will avoid the necessity of a conservatorship and the maker can prescribe his own rules for the management of the trust funds, how and for what purposes the money is to be spent, and who is to be the trustee. In addition, the trust can continue beyond the time the child comes of age so that he can mature and gain experience in the management of property before it is distributed to him. Further, the final distribution need not be all at once but can be made in installments, enabling the child to assume the responsibility in stages.

Dying Without a Will—Who Handles the Estate

If a personal representative is to handle the administration of the decedent's estate but is not named in a will, Colorado law provides a list of persons with priorities from which the court will select one individual. The duties of the personal representative (called "executor" if there is a will and "administrator" if there is no will) are to locate all of the property of the decedent;

manage it during the period of administration; pay all debts, taxes, and costs of administration; and distribute what is left according to the will or the laws of intestate succession. A personal representative may or may not be the person the decedent would have selected for the job. It does not have to be the surviving spouse or even a member of the decedent's family and it might even be a creditor. By making a will, the testator can choose the person he feels is best qualified to do to the job.

Each Spouse Should Have a Will

It is important for each spouse to have a will. Failure to properly plan the estates of both spouses may result in unnecessary expenses being incurred and may cause the loss of the opportunity to enjoy significant tax benefits which may be taken advantage of only while both spouses are alive. Prudent estate planning dictates that the problems of dying without a will be addressed for both spouses. One will alone does only half the job of planning for the family.

Dying With an Outdated Will

Colorado law makes special provision for children born or adopted after the execution of a will by their parent. Those children receive a share in the estate equal in value to that which they would have received if the parent died without a will, unless: (a) it appears from the will that the omission was intentional; (b) when the will was executed the parent had one or more children and devised substantially all of his estate to the other parent of the omitted children; or (c) the parent provided for the omitted children by transfers outside the will and it is shown that the transfers were intended to be in lieu of a provision in the will.

If a person marries after signing his will but fails to provide for his new spouse, the omitted spouse is entitled to receive the same share of the estate as if the decedent left no will, unless it appears from the will that the omission was intentional, or the decedent provided for the spouse by transfer outside the will and it is shown that the transfer was in lieu of a provision in the will.

Divorce—Its Effect on a Will

A divorce by the maker of a will affects the provisions of the will. It automatically eliminates from the will of each divorced spouse all provisions affecting the other spouse unless the will expressly provides otherwise, or the maker remarries the former spouse. If a person is divorced and dies before remarrying and updating his will, the portion of the estate he designated to go to the former spouse will not pass to her. Rather, this portion will be distributed as if his spouse failed to survive him.

Everyone Should Have an
Up-to-Date Will

Even though a person has a properly drawn will that is kept in a place where it can be found at his death, it will be of little value to the beneficiaries if it is not up-to-date. Parenthood, grand-parenthood, divorce, changing needs of beneficiaries, change of residence, sale or other disposal of property mentioned in the will, unavailability of a personal representative or trustee, gifts, newly acquired assets, and a change in the size of the estate are all indications that the will needs to be reviewed by the maker's lawyer. An out-of-date will that no longer fits the maker's desires or the needs of the beneficiaries is little better than no will at all.

Dying without a will rarely, if ever, provides a satisfactory substitute for the making of a will. Without a will a person has no choice as to who will administer his estate, who will be the guardian or custodian of the estate of minor children, or who will receive the property, in what proportions, and when. A will assures the maker that his property goes to the persons he wants it to and in the manner he desires. He can name a personal representative of his estate, a guardian, a custodian, or a trustee. A will also allows the maker to choose the sources from which debts, expenses of administration, and taxes are to be paid. Further, it can save money in court costs, guardian's fees, conservator's fees, and attorney's fees. But even more important are the savings to the family in time, worry, and court appearances and the assurance to them that the maker planned for their continued well-being. A will, very often, is the most important legal document that a person ever executes. It, therefore, deserves thoughtful consideration and skillful preparation.

Summary

A carefully prepared will containing all of the provisions necessary to transmit property from the maker to those he wants to receive it can be a real legacy in itself. Such a will relieves the surviving family of the many problems created by a will improperly prepared or no will at all. It seems, then, that each thoughtful man and woman owes a duty to his or her family to have a carefully prepared will in keeping with present family circumstances.

12

What Should My Will Contain?

A well-drafted will is tailored to the individual needs and circumstances of the person who signs it. An ideal provision in the will of one person might be unfit, and even dangerous, if used in the will of another. Nevertheless, there are numerous provisions that are included in most wills, as well as various problems that should be considered in the drafting of any will.

Introductory Provisions

A will should set forth the county and state of residence of the person who signs it. A new will does not revoke a prior will unless the new will either contains an express revocation or contains wholly inconsistent provisions. Therefore, the testator should state that this is his last will.

Appointment of a Personal Representative

A personal representative is a person or corporation who, after the death of a testator, carries out the instructions in a will, pays the debts, and protects and manages the property until it can be delivered to the beneficiaries. A will may appoint a single personal representative or designate two or more persons or corporations to serve jointly as co-personal representatives. The personal representative does not have to live in Colorado to be eligible to serve. If the will does not appoint a personal representative, all of the beneficiaries under the will may, with the approval of the probate court, jointly designate a person to serve as personal representative, or the court will select someone to serve as personal representative. To avoid the costs of a court appointment and insure that the property will be handled by someone the testator trusts, the testator should appoint a personal representative in his will. It is also desirable that the will name one or more alternate personal representatives in case the person first named as personal representative or alternate personal representative is unable or unwilling to serve.

If requested by a person having an interest in the estate, and if the court agrees that it is desirable, the probate court may require that the person named as personal representative furnish a bond to guarantee the faithful performance of his duties. The cost of such a bond will be paid out of the testator's estate. If a testator desires to avoid this cost he should specify in the will that the personal representative need not give bond since this may cause the court to dispense with the bond. Consideration should also be given to the matter of the personal representative's compensation for his services. The will may state whether the personal representative is to serve without compensation or is to be paid some specific amount or in some particular manner.

Provision for Payment of Debts and Taxes

Even if a will does not contain instructions to pay debts and taxes of the testator, a personal representative has a general duty to do so. Nevertheless, wills ordinarily contain such instructions, and there is value in this because the testator can spell out his exact wishes about debts and taxes. If, for example, the testator is making installment mortgage payments on his home, he may wish to have his personal representative pay off the mortgage in full upon his death, or he may want the personal representative, and thereafter his spouse or some other beneficiary, to continue the installment payments. If continuing the installment payments is desired, the will should say so.

Regarding tax payments, the testator may intend that certain property shall be inherited tax free with the taxes paid out of other property in the estate, or he may want the person receiving the property to pay the death taxes on it. A will should address this issue, rather than leaving it for the personal representative or the courts to determine.

The basic Colorado inheritance tax has been repealed for heirs of those persons dying on or after January 1, 1980. The amount exempt from federal estate taxation has been increased so that if the staggered increases scheduled to go into effect annually until 1987 are actually implemented, it may be possible in 1987 for up to $600,000 to pass free of any death taxes. While these changes are quite significant, it does not eliminate the need to consider the proper source of payment of death taxes for larger estates.

Provisions Disposing of the Property

The principal provisions in most wills are those which set forth to whom and in what manner the testator's property shall pass upon his death. In some states the law requires that a person leave a specified proportion of his property to a spouse, and the courts will give such property to the spouse even if the will does not so provide. Colorado does have such a requirement. However, this right may be waived by a spouse during lifetime by a valid marital property agreement. Other than a spouse, a testator may leave his property to anyone—relative or not—for a good reason, a bad reason, or no reason at all.

Likewise, a testator has great freedom of choice in determining *how* his property shall go to the persons named in his will. He can give the property outright; he can put the property in a trust;

or he can give the property on condition that the person receiving it do, or refrain from doing, whatever the testator specifies. Similarly, he can provide that the person receiving the property is to enjoy it only during his lifetime (or for a certain period of time), and that thereafter the property will go to another.

There are certain technical restrictions upon a testator's power to dispose of his property by will. For example, he must not try to control the property for too long, and he must not direct that it be used for an unlawful purpose or for a purpose that violates so-called "public policy." However, subject only to such restrictions, a testator can and should have his will written so that his property will be disposed of in the exact manner he desires. The aim of the lawyer who writes the will should be to find out what the testator wants to do with his property and then to word the will so that it carries out those desires as fully as possible, keeping in mind tax consequences.

Because a testator has such wide latitude in determining how the provisions of his will are to be written, only a few general comments need to be made about them. First and foremost, the will should be written so that it covers *all* of the testator's property. If this is not done, costly court proceedings may be necessary regarding the omitted property. To guard against an omission, a will should always contain a catch-all provision which provides that all property of every kind that has not been disposed of by other portions of the will shall go in a specified manner.

If a testator is putting his property into a trust, or is otherwise tying up its future use and enjoyment, he should be sure to consider whether he wants his home, its furnishings, his automobile, and his personal effects to be included with the other property, or whether he wants his spouse or some other beneficiary to have free and unrestricted ownership of those properties.

The pattern of many wills is to direct that specific pieces of property or sums of money shall go to certain persons, and then to follow up these specific bequests with a general bequest in which the rest of the property is left to others. Thus, a testator may give a shotgun to a friend, a sum of money to a faithful employee or charity, a farm to a certain relative, and so on, with those portions of the will being followed up by a general provision giving the rest of his property to his spouse or children.

Colorado allows the personal effects of the testator, such as furniture, antiques, jewelry, and the like, to be distributed according to a written list which is not a part of the will. This permits change or additions to such gifts without the cost of continually amending the will. The will must make reference to such a list, and there are some basic rules which should be followed in making the list.

Usually the persons who are to receive the rest of the property are the ones whom the testator is most interested in benefiting. A common danger in this type of will is that circumstances may change between the time the will is signed and the time the testator dies. As a result the will may do exactly the opposite of what the testator intended and deny benefits to the very persons whom he wished most to benefit. For example, say a testator had property worth $300,000 in 1982, when he made his will. He wanted his spouse and children to receive the biggest part of his estate, so he worded his will so that five friends or relatives will each receive $5,000, with the rest of the estate going to his spouse and children. However, if his estate has shrunk to $25,000 by the time he dies, the $5,000 bequests will use up the entire estate and, even though the testator intended for his spouse and children to receive most of his property, they will get nothing.

Consequently, whenever a testator is thinking about making specific bequests and then leaving the bulk of his estate to those dearest to him, he should always keep in mind that a decline in the value of his estate may result in its being used up by the specific bequests. One way to prevent this is to make the specific bequests in terms of fractional parts or percentages of the estate rather than in terms of dollars and cents. Thus, in the example previously cited, the testator with an original estate of $300,000 should have made the five specific bequests by giving each person $1/20$ of his estate, instead of giving $5,000 to each. Then, when the estate had shrunk to $25,000 the five specific bequests would require only $6,250 of the estate, leaving $18,750 for the spouse and children.

Provision for Alternate Disposition of the Property

When a testator provides in his will that most of his property shall go to a certain person, it ordinarily is wise for him also to provide for a secondary beneficiary in the event that the first person dies before the will takes effect. Many people want to make a chain of alternatives by providing the property shall go to "A, but if he is dead, then to Mrs. A, but if she is dead, then to B," and so on. While it is not practical to provide a long chain of alternative dispositions, it is advisable to have a final beneficiary that will certainly exist at the testator's death, whether a group of persons ("my heirs at law") or an entity such as a charity.

Provision for Common Accident or Successive Deaths

It is not unusual for a husband and wife to be killed as the result of a common accident or under circumstances that make it difficult to determine who died first. Because the husband's will usually provides for the wife to take some or all of his property, and vice versa, this type of accident can lead to serious problems.

Suppose a husband's will leaves all his property to his wife, with an alternate gift to his parents in the event that she dies before he does, and the wife has left all of her property to the husband, with an alternate gift to her parents. Then, in a common accident the husband dies first and the wife dies a week later. Immediately upon the husband's death, title to his property will go to his wife; and a week later, when the wife dies, title to the property will go to her parents, eliminating his family entirely. Such a double passage of title within a week could also result in the levying of federal estate taxes and probate administration of the property twice.

Some lawyers use a clause requiring each beneficiary to survive by a specified period of time such as 30 days, although delays are permitted up to 6 months under federal tax regulations.

The Colorado Probate Code requires a beneficiary to survive by 120 hours in order to inherit property. This amendment can be overridden by a specific provision in a will.

Other problems can arise if a husband and wife have wills of this kind, and both die from the same accident but it is not known with certainty who died first. The husband's parents may claim the property by asserting that the wife died first, with the wife's parents arguing the contrary. An expensive lawsuit may be required to settle the dispute. Also, when one of the spouses owns most or all of the couple's property, the order of death may be important in determining the tax consequences of the estate plan. A common provision in the wills is to create a presumption that the spouse with the greatest wealth survived the other spouse.

Powers for the Personal Representative

So that he can administer the estate with the least amount of time, trouble, and expense, the personal representative should be be given broad powers. Special wording should be used in the will to provide those powers. Although the Colorado Fiduciaries Powers Act gives broad powers to the personal representative unless express limits are contained in the will, those powers should be specifically enumerated and set out in the will so that there is no doubt that they will be available in a state other than Colorado where such powers are not granted by such a statute.

Provision for Guardianship and Conservatorship

When the testator has minor children, the will should appoint for his children the guardian of the person to serve should the other parent die before the will takes effect, or should the other parent fail or cease to serve as guardian for any reason. The guardian is the person who assumes the parent's responsibility for the care and education of the minor child. The will can also appoint a conservator of the property of minor children. This is the person having the responsibility for the care and management of the assets of the minor children. The guardian and the conservator need not be the same person. In some cases, it might be appropriate to have a friend or family member appointed as the guardian and a bank or trust company appointed as the conservator. A child over 14 years of age may select his own guardian, subject to court approval. But for the guidance of the court, it may be wise to name a guardian in the will, even if the child is over 14.

Contingent Management Provision

A minor child does not have the legal capacity to manage his own property. The parent of a minor child cannot legally manage the minor's property for him without court proceedings, probably a guardianship for the property, which can be cumbersome and expensive. For this reason, provisions should be made in the will to avoid the need for creation of a guardianship for any property passing under the will to a minor child. The will may create a trust for minor children or the will may provide that property that any minor child would otherwise take outright will pass to a custodian for the minor under the Colorado Uniform Transfers to Minors Act. The personal representative of the estate can then appoint the guardian of the person of the minor or an adult member of the minor's family to serve as the custodian to manage the minor's property until he reaches 21 years of age.

Required Formalities

A will must, of course, be signed by the testator. Unless it is entirely written and signed in his own handwriting (called a holographic will), it must be signed by at least two witnesses. Although Colorado law does not prohibit it, a beneficiary named in the will should not sign the will as a witness. In the usual will the signature of the testator is followed by a clause reciting that he declared the instrument to be his will, and that the two witnesses have signed the will at his request and in his presence. This clause is then followed by the signatures of the witnesses.

"Self-Proving" Will

The cost and inconvenience of probating the will may be reduced if the testator and the witnesses make the will "self-proving" by each signing an acknowledgment and affidavit before a notary public. However, this formality is not required, and a will is perfectly valid even if it is not signed before a notary public if it is signed by the required number of witnesses.

Summary

In Colorado, a testator has an almost unlimited freedom in determining to whom and how his property shall go upon his death. His will should be "tailor-made" to carry out his wishes and meet the individual needs and circumstances of his estate. However, unless certain formalities are observed and certain common problems are considered, the desires of the testator may be frustrated; the beneficiaries names in his will may get nothing or may receive an estate greatly decreased by unnecessary and costly administrative expenses, death taxes, income taxes, and litigation.

13

Pitfalls in a Homemade Will

It is known among lawyers that testators who make their own wills often create disputes that only costly litigation can settle. A testator who decides to make his own will no doubt thinks he is saving the fee for preparing the will. Perhaps his philosophy is like that embodied in the following instrument:

"Terrell Tex Jan 12—1950

"this Letter is Written With the idea that Some thing might happen to me. that I would be wiped out Suddenly if this Should Happen my business would be in awful shape no relatives, nobody to do a thing So, this is written to have my affairs wound up in a reasonable way in case of my Sudden Death. Would Like to have all of my affairs, Cash all assets including any Bank Balance turned over to Parties named below With out any Bond or any Court action that can be avoided. they to wind up my affairs in any way they See fit.
U. C. Boyles Refrigeration Supply Co.
Charlie Hill Superior Ice Co
Should these Gentleman need a third man Would Suggest Walker.
National Bank of Commerce Each of these Gentleman to receive $500.000 for his Services
I have tried to make my wishes plain. of Course these Crooked Lawyers Would want a Lot of Whereas and Wherefores included in this.
not much in favor of the organized Charities they are too Cold blooded also

not much in Favor of any person over 21—Benefitting by my Kick off unless there is a good reason
am inclined to play the children they are not Responsible for being here and cant help themselves

"Terrell—Feb. 7—1950

have Let this Letter get cold and Read it again—to See if it Seemed abut Right
dont See much wrong except no wheres and Wherefores—excuse me

Lon Gresham"

The testator would turn over in his grave if he knew that the instrument in which he had tried to make his "wishes plain" required two trips to the Supreme Court of Texas and excursions through several lower courts to fathom its meaning and consequences.

It is easy to laugh about some of the obvious problems in a will such as Gresham's, but many times learned people make errors just as costly when they draw their own will without legal counsel.

Is It a Valid Will?

One of the problems involved in the Gresham will was determining whether it was a will. If you read it carefully enough, you might begin to wonder if any property was actually disposed of and if it appointed executors. The courts were divided on whether the instrument was a will. Ultimately the Supreme Court of Texas held that the instrument was a will which disposed of no property but appointed executors to administer the estate.

Often testators leave letters (sometimes even on the back of a match folder) expressing a thought that something should be done upon their deaths. The courts may have difficulty deciding whether such a writing was intended to be the author's last will and testament or was simply the expression of a wish or hope.

The Holographic Will

There are two kinds of wills which the layman may attempt to make for himself. One, a "holographic" will, is wholly in the maker's handwriting and is valid in Colorado (contrary to the law of some other states). The other is one that is typed or otherwise not wholly in the handwriting of the testator. Such an instrument must be executed in accordance with certain prescribed legal requirements or it is void. If a purported will is partly handwritten and partly typed, it is valid only if properly signed and witnessed.

Was It Properly Executed?

One of the dangers of a will written without professional advice is that the maker may not give sufficient attention to the legal requirements for a valid execution of a will. If these requirements are not followed, the writing cannot be admitted to probate as a will. In Colorado there must be at least two competent witnesses to a non-holographic will who must subscribe their names on the will in their own handwriting, in the presence of the testator after the testator has signed the will.

Colorado also provides for what is called a "self-proving" affidavit to expedite proof of proper execution of a will when it is offered for probate. The use of such an affidavit is voluntary. If it is used, it must be properly signed and sworn to by the testator and the witnesses before a notary public or other authorized official at the time of execution of the will or later while the testator and the witnesses are still alive. The form of the affidavit is prescribed in the Colorado Probate Code.

Even in formal probate proceedings, a self-proved will may be admitted to probate without the testimony of the subscribing witnesses (who may have died or left the country), and no further proof is necessary.

Where Is the Will? Are the Witnesses Available?

One of the reasons for executing a will in a lawyer's office is that he provides witnesses who will be available for testimony at a later date if they are needed. He will complete a copy of the will by filling in the date, names of the testator and witnesses and will retain it in his office to evidence the contents of the original will itself as a safeguard should it be lost or destroyed.

Ambiguity

One of the great problems involved in a do-it-yourself will is ambiguity. The central question is: what did the testator really intend? Lay persons write in a manner which is clear to them but may be ambiguous to lawyers and judges. Here are some examples that could lead to costly litigation and end up actually frustrating the intent of the testator.

Everything to the Wife—What's Left to the Children. An expression which is sometimes found in a will written without legal advice is: "I give my wife everything I have, and upon her death I give what is left for the benefit of my children." Problems are created by such phrasing. Does the wife get the property, or only the right to use it for life? May she sell, mortgage, or lease the property, and if so, how may she invest the proceeds of sale? What happens if the wife mingles the husband's property with her own (including what she may acquire after his death)? Can she give the property away during her lifetime? Ordinarily, the words "for the benefit of" create a trust. Is a trust created for the children? If a trust is created, who is the trustee, and what are the terms of the trust? When does the trust come to an end? These are merely some of the questions raised by such wording.

Gift of Money; Gift of Land. If a testator states, "I give $25,000 to my three sons," does he mean $25,000 to be divided among the three sons, or does he mean $25,000 to each? If he declares "I give all my land in Jefferson County to my son," and the land is subject to a mortgage, does the son have to pay the mortgage or is it paid by the estate?

"Money on Deposit in Bank." Another type of ambiguity is that involved in a gift of money on deposit in a bank. Does the statement "I leave the money on deposit at the Fourth National Bank" mean only what was on hand when the will was made (say $1,000) or when the decedent died (say $25,000). And if it turns out that at his death there are two bank accounts, a checking account he had when he made his will and a savings account he opened later, who gets what?

Gifts of Shares of Stock. Suppose a testator gives to a beneficiary $1,000 or 10 shares of XYZ stock (worth $100 per share at the time of the making of the will). What does the personal representative do if the XYZ stock is worth $500 a share ($5,000) at the testator's death? Does the beneficiary have his choice?

Another recurring problem is the gift of a specific number of shares of stock without reference to stock splits or stock dividends. For example, the testator may give 100 shares of XYZ stock, this being all of the shares owned at the time of the making of the will. Later, a stock dividend of five shares for each one of the original 100 shares is declared. If the provision is interpreted literally, the recipient of 100 shares would have only a fifth the number of shares which the testator may have intended.

Gift of a Business Interest. Consider the following statement: "I give my business to my son." What happens to the accounts receivables, the inventories, the cash in the bank and other assets belonging to the business? What if the business is located on a piece of land owned by the testator; who gets the land?

Is It Tailored to the Testator's Needs?

One of the real advantages of obtaining professional advice about what to put in a will is that such discussion helps the testator decide what his basic desires are, what he wishes to do with his property, and what alternatives are available to him to achieve his objectives. Thus, he will more carefully consider the nature and extent of all his assets, the possible ways in which he can aid his family, friends, business associates, and charitable interests. He may be made aware of possibilities that he had never considered before.

For example, if he merely wills his property to his wife or to his children, he may fail to provide properly for the continuation of a business or the handling of a partnership interest, or in some other way handicap his surviving business associates. All of these things can be specifically handled in the will or otherwise during his lifetime in a way that combines the greatest amount of benefit for his family with the least amount of disruption by his death. Often such matters are overlooked by a person making his own will or complicated by incomplete or ambiguous dispositions.

Does It Unintentionally Disinherit Family Members and Others?

If a testator prepares his own will, he may fail to provide for certain persons he actually wants to benefit. For example, he may leave his property to his only son, or, if the son is not living at the testator's death, to his son's children. The latter event may in fact occur, and his daughter-in-law will get nothing. However she must raise the minor children who will get all the inheritance, and she must do it under the restrictions of a court-supervised conservatorship which will continue until the children become 18 years old. Such a conservatorship would require the added expense of applications to and orders from the court to do various things in connection with the estate. It would further require the filing and court approval of annual accountings, as well as a final accounting when each child reaches age 18.

Children of a prior marriage may be disinherited inadvertently. An outright gift to a surviving spouse followed by the death of that spouse would result in the surviving spouse's children getting the entire inheritance, while the children of the prior marriage would be disinherited.

Sometimes a testator writing his own will makes large bequests of money to friends or others. Such incidental bequests may leave little for the real object of his beneficense due to a shrinkage in his estate or because of a failure to account for estate liabilities.

Other Significant Omissions

Many other important matters are often overlooked in the self-made will. There may be a failure to give directions regarding payment of taxes due on a life insurance policy. The estate without the insurance may be non-taxable, but the large insurance policy could cause the estate to have to pay an estate tax. Who should pay the tax on the insurance proceeds—the individual named in the policy, or the persons entitled to the residue of the estate under the will?

The self-made will may fail to designate a successor personal representative or trustee in the event the original named personal representative or trustee fails to serve or dies. In the absence of the designation of a successor, the administration would have to proceed with an administrator appointed by the court.

Sufficient attention may not be given to the possibility of one death occurring within a short time of another. If a testator gives all his property to a surviving wife, all the property may go to her family to the complete exclusion of his family, even though there may be only a few minutes difference in the times of their deaths.

Summary

There are many reasons why it is not advisable for a person inexperienced in legal terms and consequences to attempt to execute his own will. Such wills constitute a prolific source of litigation with resulting family disputes and greatly increased costs of probate.

This poem by Lord Neaves is dedicated to those seeking to avoid the lawyers fee for preparing a will:

Ye lawyers who live upon litigants' fees,
And who need a good many to live at your ease,
Grave or gay, wise or witty, whate'er you decree,
Plain stuff or Queen's Counsel, take counsel of me.
When a festive occasion your spirit unbends,
You should never forget the Profession's best friends;
So we'll send round the wine and bright bumper fill,
To the jolly testator who makes his own will.

14

Choosing the Right Executor/Personal Representative

An executor is the person named in the will and appointed by the court to administer the affairs of a decedent's estate. Where there is no will, or where the will fails to name a person who is able and willing to manage the estate, the one appointed by the court for this task is called an administrator. With the enactment of the Colorado Probate Code in 1974, the terms "executor" and "administrator" have been replaced with the term "personal representative."

Selecting the right personal representative is one of your most important decisions. The one appointed will be your agent to carry out the wishes and desires expressed in your will. Integrity, business experience, impartiality, willingness to serve, and sound judgment should be taken into consideration when selecting a personal representative.

Duties and Powers

The personal representative's goal is to handle the estate in the very best interests of the persons who will inherit it. The personal representative should preserve and manage the estate and see to the payment of obligations. He should treat the assets of the estate fairly, impartially, and confidentially.

The powers given to a personal representative in a will may be limited to paying debts, expenses, and taxes. The powers also may be broad and include the rights of disposing of property, making a division among the beneficiaries, and operating a business.

Certain actions are necessary in any estate where there is a will naming a personal representative. Within a reasonable time after the testator's death, the will is taken to the attorney representing the personal representative, who will lodge it with the appropriate court and file a petition for its probate. At that time, the personal representative should know generally the nature and extent of the properties of the estate. After the petition is filed and proper notice is given, a court hearing is held in order to prove the will and admit it to probate. However, if the will is a "self-proving" will, as discussed elsewhere in this book, it may be admitted to probate without a hearing. The personal representative then qualifies and secures authority from the court to act.

The personal representative is responsible for ascertaining the properties left by the testator as well as his debts and obligations. He must prepare an inventory of the properties to be submitted to the court or the beneficiaries of the estate. If there is a going business, he must supervise it. It is most important that the proper insurance be kept in force on the properties and that any rights the estate might have be kept intact. After debts have been paid, including whatever taxes are due, the personal representative gives his final accounting and makes distributions to the beneficiaries as directed under the will.

Whom Should I Choose as Personal Representative?

The Surviving Spouse

The surviving spouse may be capable of assuming the responsibilities of the estate. Frequently, however, the spouse is untrained in the business of probate and tax problems. Under such circumstances, it may be better to appoint a bank, a trust company, a partner, another member of the family, or a trusted friend as personal representative. Eventually, the surviving spouse will be expected to manage his or her own affairs, but this can be done gradually as some knowledge of the problems involved is acquired. Perhaps a co-personal representative is the answer. The surviving spouse can act together with the steadying hand of one more experienced.

Banks or Trust Companies

Certain banks and trust companies have been granted trust powers. Their trust departments are strictly supervised by state and federal authorities. Many banks and trust companies through decades of experience have evolved systems and procedures that will protect the estate while relieving the surviving spouse of the myriad of details that would otherwise have been his responsibility as personal representative. Banks and trust companies may also provide the ideal neutral party if a family dispute were to arise. Their institutional nature insures longevity. As personal representative, a bank or trust company may employ the testator's own attorney and accountant in handling the estate. Instructions may be left either in the will or separately which may recommend an attorney and accountant. Alternatively, an individual personal representative may selectively employ certain banks or trust companies to perform specific tasks to ease the administration of an estate.

Compensation of a Personal Representative

The personal representative is entitled to a "reasonable fee" under Colorado law. This fee would be determined according to such factors as the experience of the person, the complexity of the estate, and any other pertinent considerations. The law in many states, and the law in Colorado prior to 1974, provides that the personal representative is entitled to rcccive a commission computed at statutory rates upon the amount of estate accounted for by him. This statutory commission covered all ordinary services of the personal representative. If extraordinary services were required, the court might allow the personal representative additional compensation. An individual, whether it is the surviving spouse, a child, or a trusted friend, although entitled to charge the same fee as any other personal representative, may for personal reasons charge little, if anything, other than actual expenses incurred.

An Alternate Personal Representative

A personal representative must, of course, live longer than the person appointing him. It may be well, therefore, not to name someone more advanced in age than the testator. The vicissitudes of life are such that an alternate or successor personal representative should be named in every will with the same powers and rights as the first personal representative named.

It is legal though not wise to attempt to draw one's own will. There are numerous pitfalls which may make that attempt to save money a most expensive mistake. This includes naming a personal representative without the proper expressions concerning his powers and responsibilities.

Powers of a Personal Representative

The Colorado Probate Code covers the powers and responsibilities of personal representatives. The Colorado Fiduciaries' Powers Act grants extensive powers in administering the estate. This avoids the need for frequent recourse to the court for instructions. The statutory powers may be broadened by provisions in the will. The will can grant the personal representative specially drafted powers to sell and lease property of the estate, to continue a business owned by the decedent, and to invest surplus funds of the estate in a specified manner. The will can also authorize the personal representative to serve without bond. Unless bond is waived in the will or by all of the beneficiaries, the personal representative (except a bank or trust company) may be required to be bonded at additional expense to the estate.

Co-Personal Representatives

The problem of choosing the right personal representative may be solved by naming two or more persons as co-personal representatives. You may not want to name one child over another for fear of the possible friction. This problem may be solved by naming two or more children as co-personal representatives or merely by naming a neutral personal representative.

It is common for a husband or wife to name the survivor as personal representative. The surviving spouse may be entirely capable of being personal representative and as such would act with the utmost in economy to the estate. However, a surviving spouse is often at a complete loss when the complex problems of modern business are suddenly thrust upon him or her. Under such circumstances, the surviving spouse might welcome the services of a friend or the trust department of a bank or trust company as co-personal representative. When a bank or trust company acts as co-personal representative, it usually maintains physical custody of bonds, securities, and other properties of the estate, subject, of course, to the right of the co-personal representative to inspect the properties and records during business hours.

Other than to pay funeral charges and take necessary measures for preservation of the estate, a personal representative cannot act until the will is admitted to probate by the court and he is appointed and qualified. There may, however, be certain urgent matters which require attention before the personal representative can formally qualify. If the deceased was engaged in a going business, it should continue to operate. If there are perishable assets in the estate, they should be protected. It may be necessary to arrange for funds to take care of expenses incidental to the operation of a going business or for the decedent's last illness. In choosing your personal representative you should consider the willingness and ability of the person or institution named to take immediate action. This includes petitioning the court for appointment as special administrator of the estate with such prescribed powers as are required pending admission of the will to probate and the appointment of the personal representative.

Telling Your Personal Representative Your Intentions

A personal representative should be consulted before being named in a will to determine whether he or she is willing to act. The proposed personal representative may be unwilling or unable to assume the responsibility. You then can ascertain the reason and accommodate the concerns or select someone else. If your will provides for the personal representative to exercise discretion to resolve conflicts between your beneficiaries, you should discuss your expectations so your personal representative will have had the benefit of your personal guidance in what could be a difficult situation. Moreoever, you may wish to organize all your papers in one location so that your personal representative does not have to hunt for them and run the risk of mishandling an asset or worse yet missing an asset altogether. Some find a simple accordian file with a separate slot devoted to each asset very helpful. After the will is prepared, it is a good practice to furnish the personal representative with a copy or to tell him where the original will is located for safekeeping.

Consider the case of John and Mary Doe. They were a married couple with three small children. John and Mary had separate wills that provided if they should die in a common disaster or within a short time of one another, their estates were to be handled by a personal representative and then a trustee for the benefit of their three children. The contingency happened, but neither John nor Mary had advised the personal representative of his nomination nor of the location of the wills. Administration proceedings of the estate were initiated under the mistaken belief that the wills did not exist.

Eventually the wills were found, and the personal representative named offered them for probate and qualified as personal representative. The administrations taken out before the discovery of the wills were closed, and the properties of the estates were handed over to the qualified personal representative. Extra time and expense could have been avoided if John and Mary Doe had advised their personal representative of the location of their wills.

Attributes of a Personal Representative

Considerations in choosing the personal representative are much the same as those for choosing a business partner. The necessary attributes may be summarized as follows:

- *Integrity.* A personal representative should have the ultimate interests of the heirs in mind at all times. This requires soundness of moral principal and character. He must be unselfish and honest in the handling of the estate.
- *Business ability.* Sound business judgment, combined with actual experience, is a desired quality. Many economies result from experience, and the testator's ultimate aim is to see that as much of the estate as possible passes to the beneficiaries.
- *Experience.* The handling of an estate requires knowledge of the rights and responsibilities of a personal representative and the ability to carry them out. With larger estates, knowledge of both income and estate taxation is necessary.
- *Availability.* The time a person has to devote to the handling of the estate depends on its size and complexity. If a personal representative is to keep the best interests of the beneficiaries in mind, he must have the time to devote to the estate. In handling

large estates, the duties may be so time consuming that an individual personal representative would have to neglect his personal business interests. In such a case a trust institution should be considered, since it has available officers and employees specially trained in handling estate matters.

• *Impartiality.* Whether the personal representative is the surviving spouse, child, friend, or a trust institution, complete impartiality must be given to all heirs under the will. Such impartiality may be impossible from a member of the family. If the testator believes this to be the case, he should consider someone outside of the family.

• *Discretion.* Handling an estate may bring a personal representative into contact with family problems which neither the testator nor his survivors want publicly aired. It is therefore important that the personal representative be a person who will conduct estate matters confidentially. It is his privilege to serve the deceased, and it is your right to expect matters that were held in confidence during your lifetime to be so maintained after your death.

Summary

You intend for the accumulation of a lifetime to be handled prudently. You should, therefore, select a personal representative who possesses sound business judgment tempered with concern for your beneficiaries.

In recent years people have given more thought to planning their estates than in the past. This is attributable to the ever growing difficulty of accumulating, managing, and preserving property. Taxation and its adverse effects are of special concern. A will, no matter how simple, should be prepared for every property owner. Preparation of the will should include earnest attention to the selection of a personal representative. A personal representative, in order to serve the estate in the best possible way must, like the operator of a successful business, have the necessary experience, knowledge, and seasoned judgment as well as the time to devote to estate affairs.

15

Jointly Owned Property

Origin

Many people believe that an ideal method of owning property is "joint tenancy with right of survivorship." Although there are advantages of joint ownership of property, there are several disadvantages which should be carefully considered. Even with the widespread use today of joint tenancies for certificates of deposit and other cash-equivalent investments, the ownership of property with right of survivorship is not a new idea. It was an early common law favorite. If two or more persons bought property and had title taken in both names, the presumption was that they intended to own it with right of survivorship. So, if land was sold to Doe and to Smith, and if neither had sold his interest prior to the death of one, the survivor owned the entire property interest. The reasoning was that when one died, his interest in the tract also died, and the survivor owned all. This was their agreement.

From a practical standpoint, the chief characteristic of joint tenancy is that the survivor owns the entire interest. The appealing aspect of it is the saving of time and expenses in probate by permitting the survivor to own the property automatically. In the early common law in England, the purpose of joint tenancy was to minimize or avoid feudal tenures or duties, the predecessors of present day death taxes.

In time, this chief characteristic lost its appeal, partly because of the abolition of the early feudal taxes, and partly because it became less desirable to have the ultimate ownership dependent on chance of survival. The owner of a joint interest could not dispose of it by his will. If he died without a will, his interest would not go to his heirs. If a joint tenant wanted his interest to go at his death to somebody other than his joint tenant, the joint tenancy had to be severed during the lives of the joint tenants.

Tenancy in Common

The presumption of feudal times changed during subsequent common law development from that favoring right of survivorship to that favoring a tenancy-in-common ownership. Now, if Jones and Fox bought land together, it was presumed that they owned it as tenants-in-common. Unlike the joint tenancy earlier favored, if Jones died, his interest would pass under his will, and if he died without a will, his interest would go to his heirs; at his death the survivor would not own any more interest than he owned before the death of his co-tenant. The chief characteristic of tenancy in common, then, is that the deceased co-tenant's interest passes as a part of his estate instead of to the remaining co-tenant by reason of survivorship.

It was subsequently the rule that if two persons bought property, as joint tenants with right of survivorship and not as tenants-in-common, or words of similar meaning showing this intent, the survivor owned the entire interest at the death of the other. It could be seen clearly by their express agreement that they intended for the survivor to take all. But in the absence of this agreement, it was felt that the ultimate ownership of property should not be determined by chance of survival.

Many states have express statutes concerning these early presumptions. The majority of these statutes provide that if parties buy property, it shall not be presumed that they own it with right of survivorship. In most states the right of survivorship is possible, but it must be clearly shown that this was the intention of the owners. This is true in Colorado.

Creating Joint Tenancy

Colorado statutes make specific provision for the creation of joint tenancy with respect to both real estate and personal property. The statutes provide that joint tenancy is created in the instrument conveying title to the property only if it is declared that the property is conveyed in joint tenancy. The classic language that is ordinarily used provides that title is being conveyed to the parties "as joint tenants with rights of survivorship and not as tenants in common." However, in Colorado, it is sufficient to simply convey the property to the parties "in joint tenancy." Upon the death of either joint tenant, the recording of a certified copy of the death certificate serves to establish the complete ownership of the surviving joint tenant.

Government Bonds

Frequently U.S. Bonds are registered in two or more names. A common method of registering such bonds is "John Doe or Mary Doe" (husband and wife). Such bonds typically do not contain the designation of the owners as "joint tenants" as required by the Colorado statute. If John or Mary Doe dies, does half the interest in these bonds pass under the decedent's will or does it belong to the survivor named on the bond? After conflicting court rulings in the several states, it was held by the U.S. Supreme Court in 1962 that the survivor named on the bond became the sole owner at the death of the other co-owner. In this test case, a husband and wife in Texas had purchased with Texas community funds bonds which were valued at $87,035.50 when the wife died. In her will, she gave her share of the community property to her son. In a suit between the husband and the son to determine whether the mother's will was effective, the U.S. Supreme Court held that the bonds belonged solely to the surviving husband. The high court held that a Treasury Regulation providing for the survivor becoming the sole owner upon the death of a co-owner was paramount to state law. The Texas Supreme Court decision which had given the surviving son half of the value of the bonds was reversed.

When a U.S. Savings Bond is registered in the name of two individuals as co-owners, either may redeem it without permission of the other. Upon the death of one, the surviving co-owner becomes the sole owner. If a bond is registered, "Richard Brown, payable on death to Richard Brown, Jr.," then upon the death of Richard Brown, the named beneficiary becomes the sole owner. The bonds are not a part of the probate estate of the first to die and are not liable for payment of the decedent's debts. However, this form of registration should not be used if the person who furnishes the purchase money wants to leave the bonds to someone in his will other than the registered co-owner.

Contrary to what may be a fairly common belief, there is no estate or inheritance tax savings in using this form of bond registration, nor in owning or holding any kind of property in a survivorship title. If the bonds were purchased with the husband's funds and registered "husband and wife, with rights of survivorship" or "payable to the survivor," the full value will be included for death tax purposes in his taxable estate. The surviving spouse will not be required to pay federal and state death taxes on the deceased spouse's share due to the unlimited marital deduction discussed elsewhere. The surviving spouse, as a named co-owner or survivor, becomes the sole owner of the bonds. The bonds are not a part of the probate estate of the deceased spouse. If the bonds are owned by the surviving spouse at her subsequent death, the full amount of the bonds may be subject to federal and state death taxes at that time and will be a part of the survivor's probate estate.

Bank Accounts

Many people fail to distinguish and understand the difference between an agency account and a survivorship account. "Joint account" is the popular term, but is misleading. The terms "convenience account" (also called "agency account" or "authorization account") and "survivorship account" should be used to distinguish clearly between the two different type accounts held in the name of two or more in a bank or savings and loan association.

There will continue to be problems with unintended results from creation of joint accounts because of lack of understanding of consequences of survivorship provisions. Competent legal advice should be sought before creation of joint accounts of significant size in which the joint party may not be the sole intended beneficiary of the owner's estate.

A typical person likely to have a bank account on which two or more are authorized to sign checks is the elderly widow who lives alone. She wants someone to be authorized to sign checks to pay her bills. She authorized someone else—a child, a bookkeeper, a nurse, or the next-door-neighbor—to sign checks on her account. The question that must be determined is whether the owner of the account wants the third person to own the balance. If so, she asks for a signature card, signed by both, which contains the express provision "as joint tenants with right of survivorship and not as tenants in common." This clearly indicates that the elderly widow wants the third party to have the funds in her account at her death. This is a simple substitute for a provision in her will.

However, if the widow wants the third party to sign checks only as her agent, she asks for an "authorization," or "agency," or "power of attorney" card. There is no intent to pass ownership of the balance to the third party. The balance is a part of the widow's estate at her death. The point is that there is nothing objectionable to the widow's giving the balance to the third party friend or relative who is assisting her in her business matters, but the problem comes after the widow's death when the question arises: "Did the widow intend that this friend or relative own what was left in the bank?"

Summary

Joint ownership of property can reduce the original owner's complete control over the property. Because he is sharing ownership, under law he will also share management and control of the property. This may not be a problem if the owners are harmonious, but the family picture can change through a divorce or family squabble.

There are no tax advantages in owning property in joint tenancy, but there can be tax disadvantages. Many people believe that by placing property in a survivorship form, it will not be subject to a death tax. This is not so. Any assets shown to be owned by a decedent, whether placed in joint tenancy or not, will be subject to estate tax if the value of all assets in an estate exceeds the value of assets sheltered by the federal estate and gift tax credit. This credit will allow tax-free passage of substantial amounts of property. The unlimited marital deduction provisions of the federal estate and gift tax statutes now allow tax-free passage of unlimited amounts of property between spouses. Parties with substantial estates, including jointly owned property, should obtain the advice of an attorney knowledgeable in estate planning before making major plans or changes in the ownership of property or its potential distribution at death.

Often the advantages of passing ownership to the survivor are outweighed by incurring death tax disadvantages, or having the ultimate ownership in a person other than the original owner of the property desired. A change in joint ownership or in ultimate disposition of jointly held property cannot be changed by a will. Before placing property in survivorship form, the owner should clearly understand the effect of sharing ownership of property with another prior to the original owner's death.

The owner of joint property should keep in mind three areas in which problems have arisen: (1) subsequent ownership and management of the property prior to the death of first to die, (2) liability of jointly owned property for debts of either named co-owner, and (3) taxation by both state and federal governments on jointly owned property. The owner of a bank account should clearly understand the distinction between a "convenience or authorization (agency)" and a "joint tenancy with right of survivorship" account. In the former, the authorized person or agent does not acquire ownership of the balance in the bank account at the death of the owner; in the latter, the survivor does acquire ownership in the balance.

16

What Is Community Property?

Colorado does not have the form of property ownership known as "community property." However, because we are surrounded by states having this form of ownership, and due to the mobility that exists today, many persons living in Colorado may have transported community property with them when moving here. Colorado does recognize the existence and the legal consequences of community property where its origin can be effectively traced.

The community property system is primarily derived from the Spanish-Mexican law. The system is based on a theory that a husband and wife form a "community" and that property acquired during the existence of the marriage belongs equally to both spouses. Although some of the fifty states have adopted certain aspects of community property law, only eight states currently have a fully developed community property system. These states are Louisiana, Texas, New Mexico, Arizona, Nevada, California, Washington, and Idaho. Although a common basis underlies the community property systems of these eight states, important differences exist from one state to another. Each of these community property systems is unique in many ways.

Definition of Community Property

To determine what community property is, it is first necessary to consider what it is not. Property owned by a husband or wife before marriage is that person's "separate property." Property received after marriage by gift or inheritance is separate property, as is a judgment for pain and suffering following an injury to either spouse. "Community property" is what is left. That is, community property is all property acquired by either spouse during marriage which is not separate property.

In case of doubt about the nature of a particular asset, it will be presumed to be community property and will be so judged in the absence of evidence establishing it as separate. The legal principles are simple enough, but their application can be extremely difficult, partly because the question of what is separate and what is community usually does not arise until the marriage is terminated by death or divorce. In the first case, one of the persons knowing essential facts is dead. In the second, the evidence of how and when certain assets were acquired may be tinged with bitterness and therefore unreliable.

Record Keeping and Tracing

If the husband and wife have the foresight and the financial means to establish and maintain a reliable set of records, carefully segregating separate assets and channeling all cash receipts in the proper manner, there is little difficulty in determining the character of their assets when the marriage is dissolved. On the other hand, if records are poorly kept or if cash revenues have been indiscriminately mingled without regard to their source, the determination can become difficult, even impossible. Courts will make every effort to trace a questionable asset to its source, but if there is no evidence that the asset is the separate property of either spouse, it will be presumed to be community and so treated by the court. Tracing assets has long been a popular activity for accountants, lawyers and judges confronted with questions of this kind.

Revenues from Separate Property

A large part of the trouble in distinguishing separate property from community property results from the assumption by many couples while living in a community property state that revenue from a separate asset is itself separate. Unfortunately, in some community property states, the opposite is true unless the husband and wife have entered into an agreement of the kind described in the following paragraph. Some courts have long held that income from a separate asset is to be treated as community property. This includes rent from separate real estate; delay rentals from an oil and gas lease covering separately owned real estate; salaries, wages, and other earnings of both husband and wife; interest and cash dividends on separately owned securities; and profits from the sale of separately owned livestock. Without a written agreement, the only kinds of revenues sometimes considered to be the separate property of the spouse who owns the asset from which such revenues are derived are those which represent the return of capital, such as oil and gas royalties, a bonus received for making the lease, and stock dividends and splits. A profit from the sale of a separately owned asset is usually treated as the separate property of the spouse concerned.

Agreements Terminating the Community

Some community property states provide that a husband and wife can voluntarily partition, or separate, all or part of their community into separate property. A written instrument, signed by both parties, is all that may be required. Such a partition is probably not valid as to creditors or good faith purchasers without notice until the instrument is placed of record in the county where any real property is situated. Some states even permit an oral partition.

Community property may also be converted to separate property through a gift of such property from one spouse to the other as long as there exists the requisite donative intent and the gift is not made so as to defraud or injure creditors or other third parties.

Community property law contains no provision for converting separate property to community property by a deed or other voluntary act of the parties. An attempt to do so would probably result in a tenancy-in-common. However, a "scrambling" of separate and community funds, if carried on long enough, would probably result in an eventual loss of the proof that an asset was originally separate and, as noted, in the absence of such proof, the asset will be presumed to be community.

The community estate of new community property state residents begins when their first earnings or other community receipts reach their hands. There is no automatic conversion into community property of assets previously acquired; real estate (land and buildings) in the former state, as well as personal property brought into the community property state, will remain the separate property of the owners if it was separate when acquired. But such an asset may lose its separate character through changes in form or from mingling community receipts with the separate asset.

Married persons who leave a community property state do not thereby convert their community estate to separate property. Real estate, if community property at the time of the owners' move, will remain so, and the determination whether it is community or separate is usually a question of the law of the state where it is located. Even a Colorado court would apply the law of the state in which the land is located. Property other than land follows the owner and loses some of its community attributes when the owners move to a non-community property state and become subject to the laws of their new residence.

Either spouse can dispose of all his property, separate or community, by a valid will. Indeed, it is not uncommon for the decedent to leave a will which undertakes to dispose of the survivor's share of the community estate as well as his own, perhaps substituting an interest in the decedent's separate estate for the community interest otherwise bequeathed. But the survivor is not bound to acquiesce in such an arrangement and may elect to take his or her community interest in lieu of taking under the will. Although this is sometimes referred to as "the widow's election," it is also available to surviving husbands.

Management of the Community

For centuries most community property states provided that the husband was the exclusive manager of the community, including that portion derived from the wife's separate estate or from her personal earnings. Most states have virtually eliminated the husband's exclusive management and placed the wife on an equal footing. One spouse cannot make a gift of community personal property without the other's consent, nor may one spouse sell, encumber, or convey the community household furniture, furnishings, or the clothing of the other without the other's written consent. Certain restrictions also are imposed with respect to the transfer, lease, or mortgage of community real property.

Summary

The community property system represents an equitable method of permitting the wife as well as the husband to participate in the fruits and profits to be derived from their joint efforts. All property acquired during marriage is presumed to be community property and will be treated so unless it can be shown to have its source in property owned before marriage or received later by gift or inheritance. Those having separate property and wishing to preserve its identity can do so by the maintenance of orderly records which carefully distinguish between separate principal and community income. Those persons who may wish to convert their community interests to separate estates may do so by signing a partition agreement; however, separate property may not be converted into community by agreement.

17

The Revocable Living Trust

The revocable trust as an instrument in estate planning has been increasingly popular in the past few years. A *trust* is the separation of the ownership of property into two parts with legal title (or management) of the property in one person and beneficial ownership of the property in another person. There are two broad categories of trusts—the living trust and the testamentary trust. A *living trust* is created during the maker's lifetime, while a *testamentary trust* is created upon the maker's death by his will.

Further, there are two classes of living trusts, revocable and irrevocable. A *revocable trust,* as its name implies, is one that can be canceled or changed during its existence. Withdrawal of all or any part of the trust assets can be made at any time at the request of the maker of the revocable trust. An *irrevocable trust,* then, is one which cannot be altered.

It is also desirable to know the terms used in connection with trusts. The maker of a trust is the *grantor* or *settlor.* The person or bank who is given legal title, possession, and management of the trust assets is the *trustee.* And the person who is entitled to the income and other benefits from the trust is the *beneficiary.* The following figure shows the relationship of the parties to a revocable living trust.

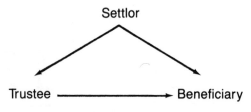

Figure 17-1. Trust Relationships.

In creating the trust, the settlor desires to provide financial benefits to the beneficiary. However, rather than transferring the trust property directly to the beneficiary, the title is transferred to the trustee to hold and manage for the beneficiary. The reasons for this arrangement are discussed in the following sections.

Terms of a Typical Revocable Trust

In the typical revocable living trust a grantor transfers property to a trustee under a written agreement. The agreement provides for the trustee to pay the grantor all of the income from the trust during his lifetime, together with such amounts of principal as may be requested by the grantor. It also provides that the grantor can amend or revoke the trust or change the trustee at any time.

Upon the death of the grantor, the trust becomes irrevocable, meaning that the terms of the trust cannot thereafter be changed. The trust property is held, administered, and distributed as if it had passed under the grantor's will through probate and into a testamentary trust. The provisions of the trust agreement which apply to the administration and distribution of the trust assets after the death of the grantor become operative and are carried out immediately. There are no probate delays, and the publicity normally necessary to the probate of a will is dispensed with.

A revocable living trust has a number of advantages and only a few minor disadvantages when compared with a testamentary trust.

Advantages of the Revocable Trust

Management Uninterrupted by Incapacity

If a bank or an experienced person is selected as trustee of a revocable living trust, and a large part or all of the grantor's assets are placed in the trust during his lifetime, the revocable trust can afford continuous experienced management of the trust assets regardless of the grantor's physical or mental incapacity. This avoids the necessity for a court declaration of incompetence and the management of the assets by a court-appointed guardian or conservator. If the grantor of the trust desires to retain investment control of the trust assets, the trust agreement can provide that while the grantor is alive and remains competent, no purchases or sales of the trust assets or any other important actions can be made without his approval. Should the grantor become unable to manage his assets, either through mental or physical disabilities, the revocable trust is the ideal instrument for continuing proper management.

In contrast, a power of attorney given to another person to manage the grantor's affairs will be automatically revoked upon the grantor's mental incapacity unless the power of attorney is a "durable power of attorney" as described in Chapter 20. Also, the power of attorney will be automatically revoked upon the appointment and qualification of a guardian. Proceedings for the appointment of a guardian for the property of a person upon his becoming senile or incompetent, or upon his drifting in and out of lucid mental periods, can provoke unpleasant family quarrels. It certainly will involve court control of the assets of the incompetent, large legal and bonding fees, severe restrictions on investments, and much red tape.

The revocable living trust is the answer to these problems. The trustee can perform all of the necessary management of the trust assets, including the collection of income, the purchase and sale of trust assets, and the management of a closely held business or real estate. In addition the trustee can make payment of hospital, nursing and doctor bills, and other expenses of the grantor. When the period of temporary crisis ends, the trust can be revoked by the grantor if he so desires, or the grantor may again take up active management of his trust assets while leaving the assets with the trustee. If the grantor dies, the trust can act as the grantor's will insofar as the assets of the trust are concerned.

Management for the Busy Executive or Professional

A revocable trust is a valuable aid to the busy executive or professional person who does not have time to study the stock market or to do the many other things that are involved in managing the investment of valuable trust assets. A bank or other experienced trustee can supply experienced investment guidance and free a busy executive or professional person from worries that might interfere with the pursuit of his business or profession, while at the same time assuring him of continuous expert investment management of his trust assets.

Segregation of Assets

A revocable trust also has the advantage of preventing certain properties from becoming mingled with other property. For example, if a wife has inherited property from her parents, and she desires that the property be kept separate from the property of her husband, she can place her separate property with a bank in a revocable trust. The trustee can maintain adequate records to keep that property segregated from the husband's assets.

Trial Run for the Trustee

The revocable living trust allows the grantor to observe the operation of the bank or person that he desires to manage his estate upon his death. The grantor can then satisfy himself as to the manner in which his assets will be managed and administered after his death. This will also allow his wife to become familiar with his trust officer and lawyer, so that old friends, instead of strangers, will be there to take care of his wife at his death. If the wife is to become the trustee upon the death of her husband, she will be able to familiarize herself with the operation of the trust while the husband is available to assist her.

Privacy of Disposition of Assets at Death

Another advantage of the revocable trust is the privacy afforded the grantor for the disposition of his estate at his death. Assets placed in a revocable living trust do not become a matter of public court record as is the case with a probated will. Newspaper publicity about the grantor's assets, his beneficiaries, and his disposition plans are thus avoided.

Reduction of Probate Expense

A revocable living trust may result in the reduction of probate expenses. Executor's commissions, attorney's fees, accounting fees, appraiser's fees, and other charges arising from the administration of a deceased person's estate are required by statute to be reasonable, but to a certain extent are based on the value of the assets passing under the decedent's will. Keeping property out of the probate or testamentary estate of the grantor can reduce such charges. If all of a grantor's assets are in a revocable trust at the time of his death, it may not be necessary to go through probate at all. However, if a bank or non-family member is the trustee, this reduction may be offset to some degree by the cost of the trustee's administering the trust assets during the grantor's lifetime. When the grantor owns property in more than one state, the avoidance of multiple probates can save substantial fees that would be duplicated in each state where property was located.

Avoidance of Will Contest

A revocable trust is less vulnerable to attack by disgruntled heirs than is a will. It is rather easy for a relative to attack the probate of a will, even when the attack is based on flimsy reasons. It is quite expensive and time consuming for the executor to win a total victory in such a contest.

An attack can be made on a revocable living trust on the same grounds used to contest a will (lack of capacity or undue influence). However, such a contest does not tie up the trust assets in the same manner as a will contest ties up the probate assets. The burden of proof seems to lie more heavily with the trust contester, as the attacks are more often successful with wills than with living trusts. The reason for this is that a will is merely a piece of paper until the testator's death. Nothing in a will has any effect or substance until after the will has been admitted to probate by a formal court order, and all assets are tied up until the will is settled. By contrast, a trust is in full force and effect at the moment of death of the grantor, and if there is a contest of the trust, the trustee has assets in his hands with which to pay for a defense of the trust.

Uninterrupted Management at Death

A revocable living trust provides a means for avoiding any interruption in the management of the trust's assets upon the death of the grantor. Stocks, securities, real estate, and so on can continue to be managed, and debts, expenses of last illness, funeral bills, taxes, and so on can be paid without interruption. Further, there is no delay incurred in providing for the grantor's family immediately after his death. This elimination of delay is important when the trust property consists of assets which require day-to-day handling to avoid loss, and when the family has immediate financial requirements upon the death of the grantor.

Avoidance of Probate in Other States

If the grantor owns property physically located in different states, it may be possible to avoid expensive and time-consuming probate proceedings in these states by conveying the property to a trustee during the grantor's lifetime. However, if real estate in other states is to be placed in a revocable living trust, it is important to make sure that the laws of the state where the property is located allow a trustee from another state to act within that state.

Tax Treatment of the Revocable Trust

Assets in a revocable living trust are taxable under the federal income tax, estate, and gift tax laws, and the Colorado estate tax laws in the same manner as property owned outright by the grantor. No gift tax is payable when a grantor creates a revocable living trust. During his lifetime, all of the income of the trust is taxed to him, and upon his death, all of the property in the trust is included in his estate for federal estate tax purposes. After his death, the trust becomes irrevocable, and the same tax advantages available to a testamentary trust are available to the living trust. These include the use of the new unlimited marital deduction or the avoidance of a second federal estate tax upon the spouse's estate, and the advantage of providing several different tax entities for federal income tax purposes.

Disadvantages of the Revocable Trust

Loss of Probate Estate as Tax Entity

To the extent that assets have been placed in a living trust, the use of the probate estate as a separate income tax entity having its own tax bracket is unavailable. Often, through good planning, payment of income tax of an estate can be delayed by strategic timing on distributions from the probate estate to a trust and eventually to a beneficiary. Of course, without the probate estate, this advantage is somewhat diminished.

Limitation on Amount of Discounted Treasury Bonds Accepted at Par for Estate Tax Payment

Certain U.S. Treasury bonds which may currently be purchased at a discount can be redeemed at par plus accrued interest at the death of the owner for the purpose of having the proceeds applied on the payment of federal estate taxes. Such bonds held by a revocable living trust are redeemable only in the amount up to the amount of the federal estate tax which the trustee of the trust is required to pay under the terms of the trust instrument. Therefore, unless the trust requires the trustee to pay all or some portion of such taxes, it may be desirable to keep the ownership of such bonds in the name of the owner himself, rather than to place them in a revocable trust.

Community Property and Revocable Trusts

If community property is to be placed in a revocable trust, the wife should join the husband in the execution of the trust agreement. The existence of both separate and community property requires special planning techniques and perhaps even multiple trusts. Assistance from legal counsel having an understanding of the tax and property law differences between separate and community property is essential.

Summary

By using a revocable living trust, a person may select a trustee to manage his assets in the event he should become incapacitated, rather than having a person appointed by the court to do so. While competent, the grantor can continue to manage his assets, even though they are placed in a revocable living trust, or he may turn complete management over to the trustee. The creation of the trust during the grantor's lifetime allows him to study the management of his assets by the trustee to be sure that the trustee will handle them in the proper manner after his death. The management of the property placed in a revocable living trust is uninterrupted at death. Such continuity may be particularly important when the property managed is a closely held business needing constant attention. By placing property owned in other states in a revocable living trust, probate within those states may be avoided.

18

The Irrevocable Trust

The *irrevocable trust* is one which the grantor cannot revoke or alter. The grantor of the trust has given up the right to change his mind and has relinquished the trust property either permanently or for some specific period of time. An irrevocable trust may be created during the lifetime of the grantor, or it may result from a revocable trust which by its terms becomes irrevocable upon the death of the testator.

Why Irrevocable Trusts?

Since the irrevocable trust by definition involves a more permanent form of arrangement than the revocable trust, it seems wise to consider at least briefly some basic background information concerning trusts. A trust is simply a device in which the legal title to property and the right to control it are separated from the right to receive the benefits from it.

Historically, the need for such a separation arose from the plight of the man with property who wanted to make provision for his family or friends but feared giving property directly to them because of their inexperience in financial management or their irresponsibility. He solved this problem by placing the legal title and management of the property in the hands of a third party whom he considered responsible. He then stipulated the manner in which the benefits were to be paid to his beneficiary.

The assurance of proper financial management is probably the most important reason for the existence of trusts. Who should be selected as trustee to exercise this management? This decision is much more important in an irrevocable trust than in a revocable trust. Sometimes a person wanting to create a trust has confidence in the judgment and managing abilities of a relative, a friend, or a business associate. But such a person is not always available. Even if he is, he may die or become disabled or his time may be too limited.

The unavailability of a reliable and experienced individual to serve as trustee can be solved by the appointment of a bank or trust company. Almost every bank of substantial size now has a trust department. Although their skill in managing property and investments varies, the close governmental supervision of bank trust department activities assures certain capabilities and inspires confidence in the integrity of banks as trustees. Grantors often find the combination of a bank and an individual as co-trustees is desirable.

In addition to sound financial management, a trust offers its grantor an opportunity for added flexibility in carrying out his desires regarding his beneficiaries. Many variations are available. The classic pattern is for one beneficiary to receive all of the income for life, with the remainder paid at his death to another. The income, as well as the remainder, can be divided among several beneficiaries if that is desirable, and termination can occur at a time other than death. For example, a father might create a trust providing for distribution of the income among his children until the youngest attains age 25. At that time the trust would terminate, and the principal of the trust would be divided among the children. The variations are limitless.

Even with all the possibilities open to the grantor of a trust, he must recognize that the circumstances which inspire his decisions today may change during the term of the trust. The perfect plan of distribution which he creates today may become the straight-jacket of tomorrow when unexpected events occur. A trust which irrevocably provides for the equal division of income between two children may seem unfortunate in retrospect if one child accumulates wealth and has great income and the other becomes incapacitated and incapable of supporting himself. The recognition of our inability to see into the future has given rise to better techniques for carrying out the intentions of the grantor.

One method of allowing for the unexpected is to give the trustee discretion in distributing income. The trust instrument may provide that the trustee can either accumulate income in the trust or distribute it to a beneficiary, depending upon the circumstances at the time. The most obvious need for such a provision is in a trust for minors. The amount of money needed for the support of a minor varies greatly as he develops through the years. Usually the decision of how much income to distribute each year can be made best as events unfold. The grantor can specify in the instrument the criteria to be used by the trustee in making distributions (for example, a provision that he wants the trust to provide a standard of living comparable to that enjoyed by the person for whom the trust was created). Or, he may have sufficient confidence in the trustee to follow the often used course of allowing the trustee complete discretion. This same type of discretion can be granted the trustee with respect to making distributions out of the principal of the trust as the need arises. Often the grantor will want the trustee to be able to distribute principal to one or more beneficiaries if circumstances should indicate a need. This can be arranged in the trust instrument. He can set the guidelines for such an occurrence or he can leave it to the judgment of the trustee.

The trustee can also be granted limited or broad power to decide who among a group of beneficiaries will receive distributions of income and principal and how much they will receive. This permits making the decision at the time of the distribution, rather than trying to make it in advance.

Heavy, graduated income and estate taxes have been largely responsible for the enormous increase in the use of trusts even for moderate estates in the past two decades. The wise use of irrevocable trusts can result in substantial savings in income and estate taxes. Sometimes the saving is only indirectly attributable to the trust device itself. Often a person desiring to effect a saving in that manner is unwilling to make an outright gift to the beneficiary. Only through a trust is he able to satisfy his personal preferences and objectives in a manner which allows him to make the gift and realize the tax benefit.

Happily for some the program of trust planning which should be adopted without considering tax benefits is also the program which produces tax savings. For others, compromises may be necessary in weighing non-tax objectives with tax-savings techniques.

Most irrevocable trusts fall into the category usually called the *long-term trust*. There is also the *short-term* trust, which has been spawned almost entirely as a creature of the graduated income tax laws, and which is also a form of irrevocable trust.

Permanent or Long-Term Trusts

These trusts are an alternative to an outright gift during the lifetime of the grantor—*inter vivos*. Such a gift, if the trust is properly drawn, will remove the property from the grantor's taxable estate and thus effect the same tax savings as outright gifts do. The grantor can reserve no right to receive income or principal from the trust, or the property will be included in his taxable estate in spite of the irrevocable nature of the trust gift. Furthermore, if the grantor retains too much administrative power over the trust, either as a cotrustee or otherwise, he runs the risk of losing the estate tax savings. The safest course from a tax standpoint is for the grantor to rely entirely on an independent trustee and retain no administrative power over the trust for himself.

Broad flexibility is available with respect to distributions of principal also. The beneficiary can be given a non-cumulative right to demand each year a distribution of up to $5,000 or 5 percent of the trust assets, whichever is greater, without jeopardizing the ultimate tax savings. A standard can be set for determining principal distributions, or complete discretion can be left to the trustee. The same plan can be arranged for the grantor's children as well. In short, the law allows the estate planner plenty of room to tailor the trust to meet the individual needs and desires of a particular grantor without endangering the tax savings.

A type of tax saving from the use of trusts is the income tax savings afforded by *sprinkling trusts* and *multiple trusts.* The sprinkling trust is the trust under which an independent trustee, usually a bank, is given broad discretion to accumulate or distribute income among beneficiaries. A trust of this type is a taxpayer itself, paying tax with its own income tax return on any income not distributed.

Because of the graduated income tax rates, a given amount of income will incur the least amount of tax if it is spread among a maximum number of taxpayers. Suppose, for example, a man having a wife and three minor sons dies and leaves his property in three separate trusts—one for each son. The income and principal for each trust can be accumulated or distributed either to the son for whom it is named or to the mother. If the mother's separate property proves inadequate for her support, the income from the trusts can be distributed to her. However, if she has adequate funds apart from the trusts in any one or more years, then the income can be retained in the trusts where it will be taxed at a lower bracket. Or some or all of it can be distributed to the sons if they need it. They may be in a low tax bracket. But the important point is that the income can be divided among the mother, the three trusts, and the three sons—seven taxpayers—so as to provide maximum tax advantages while taking care of their needs. Income accumulated in a trust is taxed to the trust, but such accumulated income can sometimes be subject to an additional tax under the "throwback rules" when it is eventually distributed to the trust beneficiary.

In creating long-term trusts, the grantor should take care in selecting the trustee and in providing for successor trustees. Care should also be taken to give the trustee or trustees broad enough management and investment powers to permit flexible administration of the trust in today's complex economic environment.

Section 2503(c) Trusts

This is a form of a permanent trust designed specifically as an alternative to an outright gift to a minor beneficiary. Discussed

elsewhere in this book are the rules relating to the tax consequences of lifetime gifts. The tax laws provide for a $10,000 an-
nual exclusion for gifts "other than gifts of future interest in
property." This means that it is possible to give $10,000 each
year to any number of beneficiaries so long as it is not a gift of a
future interest. A transfer in trust with the trustee having discretion with respect to the distribution of income is usually treated
as a future interest (rather than a present interest) for purposes of
the gift tax. The annual exclusion would not therefore be available. Section 2503(c) provides an exception to this rule if the
property and the income from it may be used for the benefit of
the trust beneficiary while he is under 21 years of age, and to the
extent not so used will pass to the beneficiary when he reaches
age 21, or be payable to his estate in the event he dies before
reaching age 21. This portion of the law also provides that such a
trust will still represent a present interest and qualify for the annual exclusion even if it does not terminate when the beneficiary
reaches 21, if the beneficiary has the power to demand that the
trust terminate and be distributed to him when he reaches that
age. If the transfer is to qualify for the annual exclusion under
Section 2503(c), the trust instrument may not contain any substantial restrictions on the use of the trust property for the benefit
of the minor beneficiary.

Demand (Crummey) Trusts

Another type of permanent trust frequently used to qualify a
gift for the annual gift tax exclusion is the "demand" or Crum-
mey trust. This type of trust can be an alternative to the Section
2503(c) trust for the benefit of minor children, but it can also be
used for qualifying gifts in trust for adults. Its most common use
is in connection with gifts of life insurance policies. These trusts
are named after a taxpayer who won an important case against
the Internal Revenue Service in 1968. That case established the
general principles now relied upon and approved in many rulings
by the Internal Revenue Service. Basically, the gift tax annual

exclusion is allowed where the trust beneficiary has an unlimited right to terminate the trust by demanding the trust property, even though the other trust provisions would not allow qualification for the annual exclusion. Even though the present annual exclusion is $10,000, careful planning is necessary if the full amount of such exclusion is to be available in this type of trust. In order for the withdrawal power to qualify for the exclusion, the holder of the demand power must be given notice of its existence and have a reasonable time within which to exercise the power. The demand power is usually drafted to extend only to any annual contributions to the trust and will expire at the end of the calendar year if it has not been exercised.

Short-Term or Clifford Trusts

Our high, graduated income tax rates have given rise to a specialized type of short-term trust designed primarily to shift the income tax burden to a lower tax bracket. This trust is sometimes called the *Clifford trust,* after the famous court case involving trusts of this type.

The best example is the wealthy executive whose high income falls partly in the top 50 percent income tax bracket. He is supporting his elderly, widowed mother, who lives modestly and comfortably on $10,000 per year. In order to provide that $10,000 per year after taxes of 50 percent, the executive must produce $20,000 in income. If he could put property into trust for his mother so that the income would go directly to her and would be taxed in her own low income tax bracket instead of his, the saving would be startling.

Happily, the tax law does allow this type of savings if the rules are followed carefully. The first essential is that the duration of the trust be at least 10 years if the property is to come back to the grantor at the termination of the trust. The trust may provide for termination and return of the principal to the grantor's estate in the event of his death before the 10 years expire, provided the grantor's life expectancy is more than 10 years at the time the trust is created. It can be made to terminate at the death of the income beneficiary (the mother in our example), if that is desirable, regardless of the life expectancy of that beneficiary.

Since this type of short-term trust is not aimed at saving estate taxes, considerably more power can be retained by the grantor than with the long-term irrevocable trust. He can even be the trustee if the trust is drawn so as to prohibit his exercising certain prohibited powers, generally related to distribution of income and principal of the trust. There is an exception. If the beneficiary of the trust is a dependent of the grantor, the grantor can reserve the right to determine how much of the income will be distributed to the beneficiary from time to time, so long as any undistributed income is allowed to accumulate in the trust, to be distributed to the beneficiary when the trust terminates.

The support of an elderly dependent mother is only one example of the many uses of this type of trust for a grantor in a high income tax bracket. Children, grandchildren, other relatives, and even non-relatives may be beneficiaries. If minor children are beneficiaries of a trust created by their parent, care must be taken to assure that the income is not used to satisfy the parent's legal obligation to support the minor children. Any trust income so used will be taxed to the parent-grantor.

Finally it should be pointed out that a grantor need not be in the 50 percent income tax bracket in order to find this short-term trust device attractive. Many such trusts now in operation are providing substantial tax savings for taxpayers whose top income tax bracket is less than 50 percent.

A Clifford trust results in a gift at the time of its creation. The right to receive the income for the term of the trust represents the gift. The amount of the gift is the present value of the right to receive the trust income. According to tables published by the Internal Revenue Service and based on a 10% rate of return, the present value of a 10-year income interest is 61.446% of the value of the initial value of the trust. Therefore, the transfer of $100,000 to a Clifford trust results in a gift of $61,466.

Summary

Irrevocable trusts, created either while living or by will, are extremely useful estate planning tools, both for tax and nontax reasons. Large savings of both estate taxes and income taxes can be realized; but even more important, proper management of property and provisions for effective security for one's family often can be assured only through trusts.

19

Life Insurance

Ownership of life insurance is another method of transferring wealth to family and other heirs without the necessity of formal probate or the use of a will. It is, no doubt, one of the most commonly held and yet widely misunderstood assets.

The Concept of Life Insurance

By and large, the general concept of life insurance is easy to understand. An insurance company (*insurer*) agrees with an individual (*insured*) to pay a sum of money, in one lump sum or over time, at that person's death, whenever it occurs. The proceeds of the policy will be distributed directly to the beneficiary by virtue of the contractual obligation of the insurer, rather than through any other dispositive instrument of the insured like his will.

In exchange, the insured agrees to pay a periodic payment (*premium*) to the insurer in an amount which is mathematically and actuarially calculated to be sufficient to cover the death benefit, administration and overhead costs, commissions, and profits. The insurance company attempts to predict when its insureds are likely to die, how much profit they can make with each insured's premium payments over the years before his death and the costs associated with administering the system. This, coupled with favorable tax laws on insurance company reserves, enables the insurer to provide substantial proceeds to the beneficiaries of the insured even if the individual dies shortly after taking out the policy.

The owner of the policy (*policyholder*) is often, but not necessarily, the insured. Sometimes the policyholder is also the beneficiary, or the beneficiary is a trust established for the benefit of the insured's family or heirs. The policyholder has the obligation to make the premium payments as well as the power to decide, among other things, who the beneficiary will be, how the proceeds will be paid, and whether to borrow any cash value in the policy.

Types of Life Insurance Policies

Describing the types of insurance policies available today would require a full length book. Even then the description is apt to be incomplete, since new policies are continually being introduced.

There are two primary categories of insurance contracts, with numerous variations available. They are *ordinary* life and *term* life insurance. An ordinary life insurance policy is a permanent contract with an even (nonincreasing) cost to the purchaser based upon the age of the insured at the time the policy is first acquired. The insurer establishes a fixed price which contains a cost for the increasing risk of mortality and a cost for the savings portion of the policy, known as cash surrender value or just cash value. The cash value portion is the excess charge which affords the insured the right to a level premium payment.

Some ordinary life products require premium payments continually until death. Others are designed to be fully paid up at a specific age (for example, at age 65). In recent years, the cash value of some policies has been capable of growing so rapidly through interest allocated or dividends paid by the insurer that the incremental value is sufficient to actually pay the next year's policy premium.

A term life insurance policy is a limited duration contract which lasts only as long as the term prescribed plus any extensions or renewals. The term can vary usually from one to five years. The contract can provide for automatic renewal, discretionary renewal, or nonrenewal. Typically, the cost of these policies increases with each renewal as the risk of the insured's mortality increases. Since there is usually no cash value associated with these policies, the initial cost is substantially reduced. Ultimately the premium cost of the term policy will exceed the cost of the permanent policy. Whether the full contract price is cheaper with term insurance or permanent insurance depends on many factors including the insured's age and mortality, the cost of money, the tax treatment of the premium payment, the policy proceeds, and the various policy provisions.

Tax Treatment of Life Insurance

There are a variety of income, gift, and estate tax consequences that affect the purchase, ownership, and transfer of insurance policies and the receipt of policy proceeds upon the death of the insured.

How is the beneficiary taxed upon receipt of life insurance proceeds? Generally, the proceeds payable by reason of an insured's death are not subject to income tax whether paid to individual beneficiaries or to the insured's estate. There may be income tax, however, in some circumstances, where the policy is owned by a person other than the insured, depending upon the manner in which the policy ownership was acquired. This makes it important to carefully plan ownership by a noninsured party.

What if the insurance proceeds are paid over a fixed period of time or in a fixed amount in installments? The proceeds are still exempt from income tax, but any interest paid on the installments is taxable as ordinary income subject to a special $1,000 annual exclusion for interest payments to a surviving spouse. This exclusion should especially be examined by surviving spouses in higher income tax brackets to maximize their return.

Are premium payments deductible by the policyholder or taxable to him? A policy owned by an individual is considered a personal asset, and premium payments are deemed nondeductible personal expenses. Premiums paid by someone other than a policyholder, such as a parent, child, or friend, are considered a gift to the owner rather than income.

Premiums paid by an employer on a policy owned by an employee are considered taxable compensation to him, unless it is part of a qualified plan of group term insurance and the death benefit does not exceed $50,000.

Will the proceeds of life insurance be subject to federal estate tax? If insurance proceeds are paid to or for the benefit of the insured's estate, the proceeds will be included in his gross estate and subject to death taxes. Where the insured retained at his death any "incidents of ownership" over the policy, the proceeds will also be included in his gross estate. The phrase "incidents of ownership" has specific meaning in the tax law. It refers to such powers as the right to designate the beneficiary, to determine the time and manner of payment of proceeds, to borrow on the cash surrender value, and to transfer such ownership interest to someone else.

An insurance policy which is transferred to a third party by the insured within three years of his death is automatically included in the insured's estate. The reason for the transfer is irrelevant; the only issue is whether the transfer took place within three years of death. If so, the entire policy proceeds are included in the gross estate for estate tax purposes. However, if an insured transfers all incidents of ownership to a trust or another person more than three years prior to death, the death proceeds will not be taxable for income or estate tax purposes.

Are there any gift taxes required upon the transfer of a life insurance policy or gratuitous payment of premiums? A gift of an insurance policy occurs when the policyholder irrevocably transfers all incidents of ownership to a third party for less than full and adequate consideration. If the transfer is revocable or the donor retains incidents of ownership, then the gift is incomplete for gift tax purposes. It does not mean that the donee has no power over the policy transferred, only that a taxable gift has not occurred.

An insurance policy is valued at its fair market value as of the time of the gift. Such value will vary depending on the type of policy involved. An ordinary life policy is measured by its "interpolated terminal reserve value," roughly equivalent to its cash surrender value plus any unearned premiums. A term life policy is usually worth only the amount of any unearned premiums.

Where the gift is made of current or future premiums, the value is equal to the premiums paid.

Gifts of insurance are entitled to the $10,000 per donee annual exclusion, as long as the donee received a present interest in the gift.

Where a policy is gifted to a spouse, it is entitled to the unlimited marital deduction. In other words, no tax would be due.

Life Insurance Trust

Frequently, an individual desires to acquire a life insurance policy on himself providing for his heirs at his death but is concerned that the proceeds will be poorly managed, available to the creditors of the beneficiaries, or subject to death tax in his estate or that of a beneficiary. In these cases, the insured may elect to create a trust to own or acquire such a policy and to receive the proceeds upon his death.

Such trusts can be "revocable" or "irrevocable," depending on the purpose and planning objectives of the insured. In recent years, it has become very popular to establish irrevocable insurance trusts for the benefit of the spouse for life and then for the children at the spouse's death. Under this arrangement, an insured creates a trust that is irrevocable and therefore cannot be amended. A trustee is named to manage the trust, which is funded only with an insurance policy (or policies) and enough cash to pay the initial premium. Each year, additional cash gifts are made to fund the current year's premium obligation.

The trust provides that, at the death of the insured, the policy proceeds will be held by the trustee for the benefit of the noninsured spouse. Income is paid periodically to her, and principal is available for her health, support, and maintenance. The trust can purchase assets from the insured's estate or the spouse in order to increase liquidity to pay taxes or cover living expenses.

When the spouse dies, the remaining proceeds can be distributed outright to the children or held in trust until the children reach sufficient age and maturity to responsibly handle their portion of the funds. Again, the trust can purchase assets from the noninsured spouse's estate, so that the estate would have sufficient cash to pay death taxes without having to sell assets to outside third parties.

The unique tax advantages of this device include avoiding death tax when the insured dies (since he gifted the policy away to the irrevocable trust, presumably more than three years before death) as well as when the noninsured spouse dies (since she is treated as never owning the policy or controlling the trust). Moreover, the costs and delays of probate are avoided on the deaths of both spouses as well as on the death of any child dying before the age set for outright distribution.

Summary

The absence of any death taxes, income taxes, or significant gift taxes on the insurance policy proceeds makes the irrevocable life insurance trust an attractive planning tool. But such advantages are available only to a carefully designed and artfully drafted instrument. Community property rules do not prevent, but may certainly complicate, an effective plan.

20

The Durable Power of Attorney

Most of this book is concerned with the subjects of death and taxes. Although these are the inevitable circumstances with which most of estate planning deals, there is also the troubling possibility of a lifetime disability making it impossible for the disabled person to effectively manage his or her assets and affairs. There are procedures established under the Colorado Probate Code for the appointment of a guardian or conservator to step in and take over these responsibilities. Under Colorado law, a guardian is a person appointed by the court to be responsible for the personal affairs of a minor or disabled individual. A conservator is a person designated by the court to have responsibility for the financial affairs of a minor or disabled individual. It is possible that the same person might be designated to serve as both the guardian and the conservator, but these functions can be put in the hands of different individuals.

One of the ways to avoid the problems resulting from lifetime disability is the creation of a revocable living trust into which all of an individual's assets are transferred. Such a trust can provide for continued management of the assets by the trustee during any period of disability or incompetency. Provisions can also be made for the continued care of the disabled person's family out of the trust property. However, there may be many situations where the use of a revocable living trust is not desirable or efficient because the size of the estate is not large enough to justify the cost and complications of a trust. The use of a power of attorney may be the best way to protect against disability in these cases.

What Is a Power of Attorney?

The use of powers of attorney is not limited to estate planning. For hundreds of years, people have been using powers of attorney to authorize relatives or business associates to transact business. The person granting the power (usually called a "principal") signs a written instrument giving another individual (usually called the "agent" or the "attorney-in-fact") the authority to transact certain matters. A *general* power of attorney gives the agent the ability to do anything and everything which the principal could do. It is a complete and unlimited grant of authority. On the other hand, a *special* or *limited* power of attorney is designed to give the agent the authority to transact only certain specified acts, and there is no authority to do anything which is not necessary to accomplish the specific activity listed in the power of attorney. A power of attorney may be of unlimited duration and would continue to be valid until the death of the principal or until revoked in writing. On the other hand, the power may specifically be exercisable only until a stated date or for a certain period of time. All powers of attorney terminate upon the death of the principal.

Although the power of attorney can be very helpful in a large number of circumstances, it is also a powerful and destructive weapon in the wrong hands. Therefore, it is essential to get good legal advice about the need for a power of attorney and how it should be structured. There is always a real problem in attempting to revoke a power of attorney which has no time limits. Even though such a power can be terminated in writing by the principal, such a termination is ineffective with regard to transactions between the attorney-in-fact and third persons if the third person has no actual knowledge of the revocation. As a result, a person holding an apparently valid power of attorney can create many financial and legal obligations which are fully binding upon the principal even though the principal has made every effort to terminate the power. The only certain way to terminate a power of attorney is to physically retrieve it and destroy it.

What Is a Durable Power of Attorney?

The problem with the ordinary power of attorney has historically been that it does not protect the principal against the lifetime disability problem. In many states, and in Colorado prior to 1974, a power of attorney was by law automatically revoked upon the disability of the principal. The purpose of this rule was to protect a disabled principal from abuse at the hands of the attorney-in-fact resulting from the disabled principal's inability to effectively revoke the power. Most lay persons were unaware of this rule.

The Colorado Probate Code now specifically permits a power of attorney to be made "durable" so that it survives the disability or incapacity of the principal. All that is necessary is for the power of attorney to contain the words, "This power of attorney shall not be affected by the disability of the principal." It is also possible to have a power of attorney become effective only in the event the principal becomes disabled at some future time by having the power of attorney contain the words, "This power of attorney shall become effective upon the disability of the principal." The problem with this latter approach is that the agent, before he could use the power of attorney, would need satisfactory evidence that the principal was disabled or incompetent before third parties would be willing to accept the agent's authority. This would usually mean the necessity for having a court determination of the incapacity of the principal so that an appropriate court order could be obtained as evidence of the effectiveness of the power.

What Power Should Be Granted?

The contents of the power of attorney will depend upon the expected needs of the principal. Business and financial management are the most common powers to be included. These would include the power to buy and sell assets, to manage a business interest, to borrow money and otherwise deal with banks, to handle life insurance matters and gain access to a safe deposit box. The ability to deal with medical-related problems could be quite important. This would include the power to consent to medical treatment and operations. In the event of a lifetime disability, it may be especially important for the attorney-in-fact to have the ability to sign hospital forms and employ a wide variety of professional assistants in dealing with the health-related problems.

Delegation of Parental Powers

There is a particularly useful provision in the Colorado Probate Code for the delegation by a parent of his or her parental responsibilities to another person on a temporary basis. A parent may be going on an extended vacation and may desire to leave a minor child in the temporary custody of friends or other family members. In the absence of the parent, it might be necessary to make decisions with regard to school activities of the child or medical care and treatment in the event of an emergency. Another common situation is where a minor child goes to visit a grandparent or other relative during summer vacation, and the grandparent might have a need to make emergency medical decisions in the event of an accident or illness. The parent of a minor child can execute a power of attorney and delegate to another person any of his or her powers regarding the care, custody, or property of the minor child. The only exception is that the power may not be given to consent to the marriage or adoption of the minor child. Such a power of attorney may not be given for a period exceeding nine months. This statute can be very helpful in a wide variety of circumstances.

21

My Farm or Business

Many people have devoted their lives and energies to developing a successful business enterprise. This business operation may be a sole proprietorship, a partnership, or a closely held corporation. The business involved may include everything from farming to manufacturing. It may employ two persons or 2000. Whether the success of the individual who was the spark behind the business can survive his death will depend largely on the amount of planning that has been done for the protection of the business.

Most businessmen are so preoccupied with daily business problems that they fail to realize that all the benefits of their business may be lost to the family after death, unless proper preparations have been made for the orderly continuation or disposition of these business interests.

What are some of the basic problems which should be considered in planning the protection of the value of a one-man business at the time of the owner's death?

Sale or Continued Operation

The first consideration that must be made after the business owner's death is whether to sell the business or continue its operations. This important decision will provide the framework for planning the protection of the surviving family.

Any business, regardless of its legal form, can become paralyzed following the death of its owner. Uninterrupted production during this period is usually difficult because the individual who has been responsible for the daily operations and decisions is gone. An orderly plan for the transfer of operational and managerial control or immediate sale is essential to insure the realization of maximum values for the owner's family.

A sole proprietorship is a business in which an individual usually owns all of the assets himself. If he dies, the personal representative of the estate will usually be under a duty to liquidate the business without delay to preserve the present value of the assets unless provisions have been made in the will for the continuation of the business.

If the business is one in which the owner's personal services were the primary income producing factor, it is probably advisable to arrange for a sale of the business assets at his death. Care should be exercised in specifying which assets used in the business are to be sold, and some specific provisions should be made for payment of the business liabilities.

But if the business is one in which the owner's capital investment was the primary income producing factor, it is generally in the best interests of the family to arrange for a continuation of the business. This may be done by directing the personal representative of the will to continue the business and by providing him with broad powers to permit prompt action in exercising of sound business judgment. Alternatively, the will may direct that the business be operated in trust. It should provide for an immediate transfer and delivery of the business assets to insure continuity of operations.

A partnership is usually terminated on the death of a partner, and the surviving partners are required by law to liquidate the business and make an accounting to the deceased partner's estate. It is possible, by making appropriate provisions in the will, to continue the partnership operations with the decedent's estate or beneficiaries. The deceased partner's will should include specific directions with respect to the continuance or liquidation of the partnership.

Partnership agreements can be drawn to protect the deceased partner's interest from forced sale or involuntary liquidation. The partners should decide during their lifetimes whether to sell their interests at death or provide for the continued participation of their families. The decision to sell or continue the business operations upon the death of a partner should be incorporated into the partnership agreement and each partner's will in order to protect both the surviving partner, or partners, and the decedent's family.

The ownership of a corporate business enterprise by an individual is evidenced by stock ownership. The decision of sale or continued operation of a decedent's corporation is complex. The general considerations in selling a sole proprietorship are equally applicable here. If personal services are a major factor, a sale at death is desirable while the business should be continued if a capital investment is a major factor. In addition it is necessary to consider other factors.

The ownership of all the stock in a business corporation frequently represents a substantial part of the total value of the decedent's estate. This creates problems both as to its sale and its retention, which are probably best resolved in light of the surrounding circumstances and existing business conditions at the time of the owner's death.

Hence, the personal representative under the will should be given discretionary powers to participate in the management and operations of the corporate business. The personal representative or a trustee of a testamentary or living trust may be given specific instructions on how and when to sell the stock, whom to sell it to, and when and under what circumstances it should be sold and liquidated. These directions may be given to the best advantage by the owner, in light of his experience and judgment in the business operations, and will provide valuable guidelines to protect his business after his death.

Liquidity

Death creates a need for cash. Many businessmen operate on credit for extensive periods of time and are constantly rearranging their business financing to provide working capital for personal needs. This source of cash usually ends upon death. Yet funds must be provided for the family's living expenses, as well as for debts and various taxes.

If the business or its assets are to be sold, the terms of the sale should be structured to insure the availability of funds for debts and taxes. If the business is to be continued at death, you must plan the availability of sufficient funds for debts and taxes to make sure the business can continue and does not have to be sold.

With a sole proprietorship cash may be generated from the sale of specific assets, the maintenance of life insurance, or the borrowing of necessary funds by your executor with appropriate directions and powers in your will.

In a partnership where the partners have so agreed, taxes may be paid with withdrawals from the deceased partner's capital account. Current partnership earnings may also be available for a period after death for this purpose. It is important to designate these payments as a continuation of income participation by the deceased partner's estate so that such payments are not mistaken for payments in purchase of the decedent's interest. The partners should plan in advance to finance the purchase of a decedent's interest as well as the continued operations during this difficult transition period.

Corporate Redemption Under
Section 303

Naturally, the owners of a closely held corporation may experience great difficulty in raising cash because of the limited market for their securities. However, under certain conditions, the law permits a corporation to redeem a decedent's stock to fund funeral expenses, death taxes, and other costs of administering the decedent's estate. The corporation may provide the needed cash from accumulated earnings without adverse income tax consequences to the decedent's estate if the redemption price of the stock is equal to its estate tax value.

To qualify for this income tax benefit, the value of the decedent's stock in the closely held corporation must exceed 35% of the decedent's adjusted gross estate. The adjusted gross estate is generally the gross estate minus the debts, losses, and funeral and administrative expenses. Stock in two or more businesses may be aggregated together to exceed this 35% requirement if a decedent owned 20% or more of the value in each such business.

The redemption may be made for cash, a promissory note or other corporate property. Moreover, the funds or property withdrawn need not be actually used to pay the death tax, funeral, and administrative expenses.

Installment Payment of Estate Tax

The estate may also qualify for an installment payment of that portion of the federal estate tax attributable to a closely held business. The estate may pay interest only for five years followed by ten annual installments of principal and interest. Interest on the deferred estate tax on the first one million dollars in value of the business is 4%, and interest on the balance of the deferred tax is paid at the then-current interest rate for tax deficiencies.

Generally most businesses will qualify; however, certain kinds of activities such as management of passive investments will not. The requirement for qualification should be carefully reviewed with counsel.

In addition, the decedent's interest in the closely held business must exceed 35% of the adjusted gross estate, but two or more business interests can be combined to exceed this 35% requirement if the decedent owned 20% or more of the total value of each such business.

After a family begins the installment payments, there are still some concerns. Acceleration of the unpaid federal estate tax can occur if more than 50% of the business is sold or withdrawn during the installment period. Failure to pay either the interest or principal on any installment may also trigger acceleration.

Special-Use Valuation for Farms and Business Real Property

Property is valued at its "highest and best use" for purposes of assessing the federal estate tax. A relief provision is available in view of the inequity of valuing land used for farming or in a business at its "highest and best use" when the income it produces may be insufficient to pay the tax. The personal representative may elect to have this real estate valued on the basis of its actual use in the farm or business.

This real property must be included in the decedent's gross estate and must be "qualified real property" applied to a "qualified use" that passes to a "qualified heir." Proper planning is critical to enjoy this valuable relief provision.

A maximum reduction in valuation of $750,000 from the "highest and best use" value is allowed.

Buy-Sell Agreements

In planning it is important to accommodate the potential dynamic between the needs of the surviving family for cash to settle the estate and maintain their standard of living and the needs of the business for cash for operations. Our discussion now turns to one of the solutions—the buy-sell agreement.

This agreement is a contract which provides for the purchase and sale of the business interest, whether a sole proprietorship, partnership, or corporation. The contract is used to protect the surviving family from forced sales and depressed prices while protecting the continuing owners or operators of the business from the interference of those in the decedent's family who are not active in the business.

Buy-sell agreements may include provisions for funding the purchase price and assuring that the cash will be available to the decedent's estate. These provisions may be as broad and varied as the imagination of the business planner.

Parties to a buy-sell agreement may be found both in and out of the business. The sole proprietor may look to certain key employees who may be interested in taking over the farm or business. The same considerations would apply to one who is the only shareholder of a closely held corporation. Where there is more than one owner, the other owners may agree to purchase the decedent's interest. A competitor may also be interested in participating in a buy-sell agreement.

You should structure the sale of your business while you are alive when your family's bargaining position is greater.

The Cross-Purchase Agreement

The cross-purchase agreement obligates the estate of a deceased owner to sell to the remaining owners who in turn are obligated to purchase the decedent's interest from the estate. The parties to this agreement are the individual owners and not the partnership or corporation itself.

However, the cross-purchase agreement presents some problems. First, the surviving owners may find it very difficult to personally raise the funds necessary to purchase the decedent's interest. An installment sale can alleviate this problem to some extent. Life insurance policies which pay proceeds to the surviving owners on the decedent's death are also an alternative, but each business owner must maintain a life insurance policy on the life of each other owner. Where there are many owners, this creates the need for many insurance policies, and this can be both costly and confusing.

The Redemption Agreement

Many businesses therefore select the "entity purchase" or "redemption" agreement where the business entity (partnership or closely held corporation) agrees to purchase the interest of a retiring or deceased owner. Corporate funds can be used to purchase the interest of the decedent. A corporate redemption can be funded through life insurance with only one policy needed on the life of each owner in contrast to the multiplicity of policies required in the cross-purchase agreement.

Setting Estate Tax Values

One of the big problems of the closely or privately held business is the determination of the appropriate value for federal estate tax purposes. Understandably, the personal representative of the estate of the deceased owner tends to want to appraise the value of assets at the lower end of their range of values in order to minimize the estate tax consequences. On the other hand, the Internal Revenue Service, being suspicious of this tendency on the part of the estate, will tend to select the higher end of the range of values. Many costly tax disputes center around this question of valuation.

A properly drafted buy-sell agreement can set the value of the business for tax purposes and eliminate tax litigation. The principal requirements for a valid agreement acceptable to the Internal Revenue Service are lifetime restrictions upon sale or transfer of the business interest without the prior consent of the other business owners, and a mandatory obligation on the part of the estate to sell and the business entity or other business owners to purchase at death. A mere option to purchase at death will not be effective to fix tax values. It is immaterial that the price determined under the agreement is payable in a lump sum or by installments. Great care must be taken and professional assistance engaged to determine an appropriate formula to be inserted in the agreement for the determination of the value at death.

Summary

There are no cure-all substitutes for thorough business planning to preserve the value of a farm or business at the owner's death. Nor is there a single device by which all problems created at death can be easily resolved.

A well considered plan which studies each of the problems peculiar to the business operation of the individual is essential to preserve and protect the value of the business at death.

22

THE "LIVING WILL"

Origin

With the advances in medical treatment over the last several years, there has been an increasing controversy over the right to die when a patient has reached the point where death is imminent and inevitable. Since medical science can keep an individual in a state of almost perpetual vegetation, many individuals do not wish to have life sustained through the use of extraordinary techniques. Unfortunately, at the time when a patient is undergoing life-sustaining treatment, he is unable to express his desires because a coma usually accompanies these conditions.

Various organizations, such as the Society for the Right To Die, have lobbied vigorously for many years to persuade states to legislate the ability of patients to make a decision regarding this issue while they are still healthy and competent. This has been an emotional issue which involves religious, social, legal, and medical issues.

As of January 1985, approximately twenty-three states have enacted statutes which recognize the ability of a person to express his or her desires in regard to extraordinary medical care in the event of a terminal illness or injury. Colorado has enacted a statute called the Colorado Medical Treatment Act, which was signed into law on May 9, 1985. This law is patterned on similar statutes in other states with various provisions peculiar to Colorado.

Provisions of Colorado Law

Under the new Colorado statute, any competent adult may execute a written declaration directing that life-sustaining procedures be withheld or withdrawn if he is in a terminal condition and is either unconscious or otherwise incapable of deciding whether medical treatment should be accepted or rejected. In the case of a declaration signed by a pregnant patient, if a medical evaluation determines that the fetus could probably be delivered alive, then any such written declaration is invalid. The declaration must be executed before two witnesses and can be in the form set out in Figure 22-1. However, the declaration need not necessarily be in that precise form.

If the patient is physically unable to sign a declaration, the statute permits it to be signed by some other person in the patient's presence and at his direction. Neither the witnesses nor a person signing a declaration on behalf of a physically disabled patient can be the attending physician or an employee of the attending physician, an employee of the institution in which the patient is hospitalized, or a person who could benefit from the estate of the patient at death.

There is a rather complicated procedure to be followed by the attending physician when presented with such a declaration. The attending physician and at least one other physician must both determine that the patient's medical condition is terminal. The attending physician then has certain requirements about notifying family members of the patient. If the declaration is not challenged by those family members within forty-eight hours after the physician has signed a certificate of terminal condition, then all life-sustaining procedures are to be withdrawn or withheld pursuant to the terms of the declaration. Any physician who acts in accordance with the declaration is exempted from any civil or criminal liability as a result of the decision to suspend medical procedures.

In order to eliminate potential problems in connection with the payment of life insurance benefits where the death is a result of withholding medical treatment and death occurs within the one-year suicide clause contained in all life insurance policies, the

Declaration as to Medical or Surgical Treatment

I, ___(name of declarant)___ , being of sound mind and at least eighteen years of age, direct that my life shall not be artificially prolonged under the circumstances set forth below and hereby declare that:

1. If at any time my attending physician and one other physician certify in writing that:

   a. I have an injury, disease, or illness which is not curable or reversible and which, in their judgment, is a terminal condition; and
   b. For a period of forty-eight consecutive hours or more, I have been unconscious, comatose, or otherwise incompetent so as to be unable to make or communicate responsible decisions concerning my person; then

   I direct that life-sustaining procedures shall be withdrawn and withheld; it being understood that life-sustaining procedures shall not include any medical procedure or intervention for nourishment or considered necessary by the attending physician to provide comfort or alleviate pain.

2. I execute this declaration as my free and voluntary act this ____ day of _____, 19__.

   By _____
                                   Declarant

The foregoing instrument was signed and declared by _(name of declarant)_ to be his declaration, in the presence of us, who, in his presence, in the presence of each other, and at his request, have signed our names below as witnesses, and we declare that, at the time of the execution of this instrument, the declarant, according to our best knowledge and belief, was of sound mind and under no constraint or undue influence.

Dated at _____, Colorado, this ____ day of _____, 19__.

____(name of witness)____   Address: _____
_____

____(name of witness)____   Address: _____
_____

statute provides that following the directions contained in the declaration does not constitute suicide or homicide. In addition, the existence of the declaration does not in any way impair any life insurance contract or justify any increase in a life insurance premium as a result of the existence of the declaration.

Summary

Individuals who are concerned about the issue of the right to die now have express statutory permission under Colorado law to determine to what extent medical treatment will be extended under terminal conditions. Although an increasing number of states are enacting legislation, there are still a number of states which do not have legislation of this type. A "living will" executed in Colorado would not be valid in a state which does not have the same or similar legislation. Because of the sensitivity and importance of this matter, individuals desiring to take advantage of the Colorado law should consult with legal counsel to make certain that the declarations which they prepare are valid and will be observed at the appropriate time.

Epilogue:
A Personal View

Time

He awoke and inhaled the morning.
After bathing in the oceans
he dressed for the day.
He wrapped himself in the earth,
draped on the stars and the sky.
Then adorning those with the moon and sun
he opened the doors
to enter the world.

The cold spring morning
aged to a heated summer noon
breeding and ripening everything living.
The young Man wore creation with a smile
since summer was all he knew.

Quickly, noon gave way to
the season of decline,
When the mellow sun mocks with
a hint of winter.
He feared, and returned
to his place of awakening.

He took off the stars and sky,
the sun and moon,
and the earth fell atop
the heap on the bed.

Tightly on his arm
he bound his watch forever.
Then redonned the earth,
the stars and sky,
and the sun and moon.
And he faced the winter
with a measure for time,
to plan for what lay ahead.

Clara Ann Dufficy

162

Time. The inexhaustible commodity that you cannot buy, sell, or accumulate. It is limitless in the sense that there is enough for everyone. It is limited in that every man has only his measured portion and no more. It may be used, but it cannot be possessed. Curious that such an elusive element as time sometimes becomes the enemy of estate planning. How can this be so?

Procrastination—the thief of time—robs many people of the opportunity to successfully complete their estate planning goals. Admittedly, there are some people who do not view wealth accumulation as a goal and do not, therefore, stress its conservation or transmission. However, there are others who seem to place much emphasis on acquiring riches, and it has always surprised me to encounter those individuals who have successfully attained their goals and have accumulated great wealth but who seem to have little interest in preserving it. It is as though in the feverish activity of accumulating material things there is a loss of the awareness of our mortality. I have actually had clients die on the eve of their appointment to sign wills and trusts which had been resting in my file for many months. It is naive to assume that we have so mastered time that there will always be tomorrow.

Time also creates changes in the circumstances of life which make an estate plan outdated. A will or trust which may be proper while our children are yet minors is not usually appropriate once they attain adulthood. An estate plan which may be adequate when the value of assets is relatively nominal will no longer be suitable when the accumulated assets reach taxable proportions. The planning for a single person is certainly not fitting for a married couple. A timely tax plan can be instantly made obsolete by changes in the tax laws. I always stress to my clients that estate planning is not an *event* which we attend and then immediately forget. It is a *process* which continues to require review and alteration as personal and financial circumstances change with the passage of time.

The matters discussed in this epilog come from my estate planner's soul, rather than my intellect. The manual you have read was not written as a commercial venture. It is the outgrowth of twenty-four years of meeting with clients of all ages and circumstances. After the initial client meeting to discuss the estate planning techniques most suited to the individual seated before me, I am frequently asked for direction to a book or reading material where additional information can be found and studied. Although there are a few excellent books available, many of them contain more information than the client ever wanted to know about the subject, and the material is not specifically adapted to Colorado law. It is my sincere desire that my friends, clients, and others reading this book will find in it positive and helpful ideas for building up an estate, preserving the fruits of their labors, and transferring the unused portion to their families and other beneficiaries.

Estate planning is both a science and an art. As a science, it involves the use of tax tables, formulas, legal documents, mathematics, and purely objective techniques. As an art, estate planning is subjective. Emotional. Intensely personal. When a client comes to see an estate planner, he may have some fuzzy ideas about the desired disposition of his estate, but he generally does not know exactly what he wants. As a result, the estate planner is more than a dispenser of technical information. He is a counselor. People are the proper subjects of estate planning, not just things.

Most of the horror stories that one hears about wills, trusts, and estate planning result from poorly conceived or implemented advice by those entrusted with the secrets of estate planning. Sometimes this is because the client is not forthright and honest with his advisers. At other times, the adviser tries to cram the client into a preconceived mold. Although the great majority of people fit into a rather limited number of well-defined patterns, the slavish use of forms will surely work injustice in the unique situations.

Let me caution the reader against undue concentration on the "dead-hand" approach to estate planning. This is the tendency to control people and property from beyond the grave. Few things are personally more objectionable to me than the attempt to manipulate the lives of family and friends by the manner in which financial favors are either withheld or dispensed in wills and trusts. Obviously, it is important to safeguard property against unwise use by persons who due to age or the circumstances of life are incapable of wisely managing their own financial affairs. The danger is that we can overdo this and turn people into financial puppets.

Wealth accumulation and transmission are concerns as old as man. In Proverbs 22:3, the Bible states that, "A prudent man foresees the difficulties ahead and prepares for them; the simpleton goes blindly on and suffers the consequences." The subjects of probate and estate planning are so often associated with dying that many people strive to delay the process until the last minute and then miscalculate the amount of time remaining. Again, in those cases, time becomes the enemy.

Perhaps a philosophical epilog such as this seems out of place in a book designed primarily to convey facts and techniques. But it is my hope that this chapter of the book will focus the reader's attention on the true goal of estate planning, which is planning the lifetime care and use of property—ours while we still have time and health to use it, and later for friends, family, and charities. That is why the professional advisers who engage in the business of estate planning have such a solemn responsibility to dispense accurate and sensitive advice. And that is the perspective from which I hope you will review and utilize the information in this book.

An epilog is defined as a short addition or concluding section at the end of any literary work, often dealing with the future of its characters. In this case, the characters are those of you who have read this book. Your future includes seeking out the best avenues for passing on your hard-earned and prized possessions to those dear to you or other deserving beneficiaries. I would say, "Good luck," but estate planning is not a matter of luck at all. Instead, let me urge you to be wary of time and use the knowledge which you have gained from this book to help you plan for what lies ahead.

Glossary

adjusted gross estate: used only for federal estate tax purposes. The adjusted gross estate is the value of the decedent's estate for federal tax purposes figured by subtracting funeral and administrative expenses, debts, taxes, and certain other items from the total value of the estate.

administrator: one appointed by the court to administer the estate of the decedent. His principal duties are to collect the properties of the estate, pay the debts of the decedent, and distribute the estate to the people entitled to it. An administrator is appointed if the decedent failed to appoint an executor in his will or died without a will. The feminine form of administrator is "administratrix."

appreciation: growth in the fair market value of the property. The term usually refers to an increase due to fluctuation in the market value of the property rather than changes in the property itself. Autonym: depreciation.

beneficiary: one for whose benefit a trust is created, or one to whom the proceeds of insurance are payable.

commingling: the placing together of property of various kinds. In community property states, the term has special significance and refers to the mixing of one spouse's separate property with community property or with separate property of the other spouse.

community property: property acquired by either spouse during marriage, except by gift, will or inheritance. This is a property system based on the theory that marriage is a partnership. There are eight community property states.

convenience account: a bank account established by one person (a) in the name of himself and another person (b) for the purpose of allowing either person to draw out money to be used for the benefit of the first person. A common example of such an account is the situation in which the first person is aged or ill and is unable to go to the bank to obtain funds, so the account is established to allow a second person to draw funds for the "convenience" of the other.

court-made law: law which is established by court decision rather than by the act of the legislature. This term applies to interpretations of statutes and theories set forth in court decisions.

decedent: a deceased person. The term refers either to one who dies leaving a will or to one who dies without a will.

devise: (noun) in most states, a gift of real estate which is made by the will of a deceased person; (verb) to give real estate by means of a will. In Colorado, this term includes a testamentary gift of either real or personal property.

devisee: one who receives real estate or other property under the terms of a will.

disposition: transmitting or directing property ownership, as in disposition of property by a person's will.

durable power of attorney: a written authority for one person to perform specified actions on behalf of another, which authority is not affected by the lifetime disability of the one granting the power.

encumbrance: a claim, lien, charge, or liability against property, such as a mortgage.

estate: the entire property owned by a person, whether land or movable property. In the probate context the term refers to all property left by a decedent.

executor: one who is appointed in the will of a decedent to manage the estate and to carry out the directions in the will for disposition of the estate property. In Colorado, the testator can direct that his executor be unsupervised and relatively independent of the control of the probate court. The feminine of executor is "executrix."

fair market value: the value of property that would be set by an owner willing (but not forced) to sell for cash and a buyer willing (but not forced) to buy for cash, with both buyer and seller knowing all relevant facts. The fair market value of property is intended to be an estimate of value which is fair, economic, and reasonable under normal conditions.

grantor: a person who transfers property, other than by will (where he would be called "testator") or trust (where he would be called "settlor"), to someone else (known as the "grantee"). The term is generally used to describe the one who transfers property by gift or by sale.

holographic will: a will written entirely in the handwriting of the testator.

intestate: a person is said to die intestate when he leaves no valid will to control the disposition of his property.

joinder: joining or coupling together; uniting with another person in some legal step or proceeding.

joint tenancy with right of survivorship: generally, ownership of property by two or more persons who have the same interest in the property and own it together; all rights in the property pass to the survivor upon the death of any one joint tenant and ultimately pass to the last survivor. Thus, the interest of a joint tenant is not included in his estate when he dies, since he cannot control the disposition of his interest in the property.

letters: a document of authority issued to an executor or personal representative by the probate court showing his authority to serve as executor.

liquidity: used to describe whether an asset can be converted into cash easily. For example, stock which can be easily sold has good liquidity; stock which cannot be easily sold has poor liquidity.

personal representative: a general term which, depending upon the context, includes an executor, administrator, special administrator, or a successor to any such fiduciary.

personalty: property other than real estate is said to be "personalty." The term also applies to contract rights.

posting: giving public notice, generally by displaying a written announcement in an official, conspicuous place attaching a notice to the courthouse bulletin board.

probate: the procedure for proving to the satisfaction of the probate court that an instrument is the last will and testament of the decedent.

quitclaim deed: the deed intended to transfer whatever interest the grantor had, if he had any at all. This deed is distinguished from a warranty deed, in which the grantor guarantees that he does have a certain interest.

realty: land and mineral interests. This includes buildings located on the land as well as crops and trees growing on the land. Synonyms: real estate, real property, or immovables.

self-proving will: a will which does not require that the witnesses appear in court to prove that the will was properly signed by the testator, because after signing the will the testator and the witnesses signed an additional document (not part of the will) in which they swear before a notary public that the will was correctly signed.

settlor: the maker of a trust. The party owning property that becomes the asset of the trust, which is managed by the trustee for the beneficiary.

survivorship account: a bank account in the name of two or more persons in which the entire amount passes to the survivor or survivors upon the death of one of the owners. The account may be with a company other than a bank.

tenants in common: ownership by two or more persons of the same piece of property in which each has the right to use and occupy the property at the same time with all the other owners. This type of ownership differs from the "joint tenancy with right of survivorship," in that the interest of the deceased owner does not pass to the survivors. Thus, a tenant in common may dispose of his interest by will.

testator: one who has made a will; one who dies leaving a will. The feminine of testator is "testatrix."

trust: a legal arrangement whereby property is transferred to one person for the benefit of another person.

trustee: the person who holds the property in trust for the benefit of another person who is called the beneficiary.

valuation: the act of ascertaining or estimating the worth of the property.

Index